Acclaim for
A Season of G

"*A Season of Grief* is a beautifully crafted, candid, and extremely moving book. As Bill Valentine mourns the death of his lover, he explores the broad range of their relationship, sharing with us the high quality and integrity of their life together. We experience its complexity, stress, humor, remarkable intimacy, and deep love. In his writing, the author gives us real people in real situations. He doesn't overlook the problems all life partners encounter—these two face them, and with hard work they overcome them. We meet their friends and families, we travel with them, we celebrate Joe with them—they're amazingly vivid, they seem to enter our lives too. And we laugh as well as cry as Valentine maintains an ongoing conversation with Joe Lopes and tries to keep him close.

My husband has recently died, and *A Season of Grief* resonates profoundly for me. As I followed the author through the days, weeks, and months after Joe died, my own grieving became clearer, memories more vivid. Places and people made welcome connections to past joys. My husband sometimes seemed near, bringing reassurance about my regrets and failings, confirming our love, and blessing my reemergence into the world. My sadness for Bill merged with my own sadness, which, because it was shared through this book, seemed in part to heal. The intelligence, honesty, and insight with which Valentine examines and expresses his feelings are extraordinarily generous and caring.

I believe that *A Season of Grief* will be a tremendous help and comfort to those who mourn, and will help us all to confront and deal with our grief and loss."

—Flora Miller Biddle
Chairman Emerita,
Whitney Museum of American Art;
Author of *The Whitney Women
and the Museum They Made*

"The thread of memorializing one's lover through language is a genre within gay and lesbian literature with a history several millennia old, beginning with the poems of Sappho. With the coming of the AIDS pandemic, this type of writing became not only more prominent but also somewhat stereotyped, with the actual processes of grief blurred through repetitive presentation. *A Season of Grief* redeems this type of writing by showing in a frank and open manner exactly how difficult and many-staged the process of normal grieving is, and doing so in a context which is unrelated to either the 9/11 attacks or AIDS.

Valentine's text interweaves several streams of histories—his own, his lover Joe's (a flight steward killed in the crash of Flight 587), and the history of grieving and the awareness it brings. From bird-watching in the deserts of Texas to the streets of New York, this is an unusual and thoughtfully crafted work."

—Robert B. Ridinger, MA, MLS
Editor, *Speaking for Our Lives:
Historic Speeches and Rhetoric
for Gay and Lesbian Rights (1892-2000)*

"Bill Valentine's moving memoir explains loss by exploring love, and it tells the story of grief as a way of showing how deeply satisfying the bond between two gay men can be. In this memoir, Bill gives an account of his partner Joe's death in the crash of American Airlines Flight 587 on November 12, 2001. This tragedy is given meaning through the description of the life that Bill and Joe shared. We learn a lot about who these men are and how they achieved the degree of intimacy that the memoir commemorates. The ways in which Bill tries to recover from Joe's loss tell us as much about the man he is as about the man he has lost. As such, it is inspiring reading. This is a memoir to make us think again about who we are and who we can be."

—George Haggerty, PhD
Professor of English,
University of California, Riverside

A Season of Grief

HARRINGTON PARK PRESS®
Southern Tier Editions™
Gay Men's Fiction

A Season of Grief

Bill Valentine

Southern Tier Editions™
Harrington Park Press®
An Imprint of The Haworth Press, Inc.
New York • London • Oxford

For more information on this book or to order, visit
http://www.haworthpress.com/store/product.asp?sku=5542

or call 1-800-HAWORTH (800-429-6784) in the United States and Canada
or (607) 722-5857 outside the United States and Canada

or contact orders@HaworthPress.com

Published by

Southern Tier Editions, Harrington Park Press®, an imprint of The Haworth Press, Inc., 10 Alice Street, Binghamton, NY 13904-1580.

PUBLISHER'S NOTE
The development, preparation, and publication of this work has been undertaken with great care. However, the Publisher, employees, editors, and agents of The Haworth Press are not responsible for any errors contained herein or for consequences that may ensue from use of materials or information contained in this work. The Haworth Press is committed to the dissemination of ideas and information according to the highest standards of intellectual freedom and the free exchange of ideas. Statements made and opinions expressed in this publication do not necessarily reflect the views of the Publisher, Directors, management, or staff of The Haworth Press, Inc., or an endorsement by them.

Excerpt from "The Long Shadow of Lincoln: A Litany" in THE COMPLETE POEMS OF CARL SANDBURG, copyright 1950 by Carl Sandburg and renewed 1978 by Margaret Sandburg, Helga Sandburg Crile, and Janet Sandburg, reprinted by permission of Harcourt, Inc.

Excerpt from "A Blessing," by James Wright, from *Above the River* (Farar Straus and Giroux, 1990). © 1990 by James Wright. Reprinted with permission of Wesleyan University Press.

Excerpt from "Under the Harvest Moon" in CHICAGO POEMS by Carl Sandburg, copyright 1916 by Holt, Rinehart and Winston and renewed 1944 by Carl Sandburg, reprinted by permission of Harcourt, Inc.

Cover design by Lora Wiggins.

Library of Congress Cataloging-in-Publication Data

Valentine, Bill, 1954-
    A season of grief / Bill Valentine.
        p. cm.
    ISBN-13: 978-1-56023-573-6 (pbk. : alk. paper)
    ISBN-10: 1-56023-573-X (pbk. : alk. paper)
    1. Gay men. 2. Middle-aged men. 3. Loss (Psychology) I. Title.

HQ76.14.V35 2005
973.931'092—dc22

                                                                2005015666

To Joe,
with love, respect, and unyielding affection.

And to the crew, passengers, and ground victims
of American Airlines Flight 587,
November 12, 2001, Belle Harbor,
Queens, New York.

Acknowledgments

Malaga Baldi's support of my writing and her belief in this project made *A Season of Grief* possible. Thank you, Malaga.

Bill Palmer at The Haworth Press took a chance on an unpublished writer. I am grateful. My interactions with the staff at Haworth were always professional and pleasant. I am particularly indebted to Jillian Mason-Possemato for her early encouragement and guidance.

Throughout my season of grief I was sustained by the love and generosity of Joe's colleagues at American Airlines, his family, his longtime friends, my family, and my friends. Some of you read parts of the manuscript. Some of you appear in these pages. To all of you I can offer only my deepest thanks and tell you that you, named or not, are part of this work.

Love Story for Joe:
A Eulogy*

I'd like to take a few minutes this afternoon to talk with you about Joe, who was known to us also as Joseph, Joey, JoJo, Uncle Joe, J Lo, Sweet Pea, Honey Bun, Darling, Puss, and other names I am sure I have not yet learned.

I'm going to take my time, and I hope you won't have to wait too often for me. If necessary, I will wait for you. No awards will be given at the end for stoicism. Laughter is highly encouraged.

Music

Music was fundamental to Joe's life. He could not live without it. He had a lovely singing voice. He introduced me to the great female vocalists—Ella, Billie Holiday, Sarah Vaughan, Diana Krall, and Etta James. He loved Etta; he loved her brassiness and her tenderness. I am so thankful that we were able to see her perform at B. B. King's this past Labor Day.

My sister-in-law Heidi introduced us to Eva Cassidy a few years ago and she quickly became one of our favorites. One way to connect to Joe's spirit is to get a copy of Eva's CD, *Songbird,* and listen to her version of "Over the Rainbow."

I remember walking down the hill on Amsterdam Avenue one night and looking up into our apartment and seeing wild shadow movements. When I got home, I found Joe attached via headphones to the stereo, lip synching Aretha Franklin. He was not even aware of

---

Read at St. Paul's Chapel, Columbia University, New York, New York, December 1, 2001. Quotations are from "The Long Shadow of Lincoln: A Litany" by Carl Sandburg, also read at Joe's service.

my presence; he had passed into another world. The headphones formed an umbilical chord. Passing through the chord was music, the food and nutrients necessary to feed his soul.

His tastes could not be pigeonholed. He could belt out show tunes and "Stand by Your Man." He loved Patsy Cline. He loved Cher; he loved her beyond all appeals to reason.

But he was probably one of the few people in the world to love Cher and Gregg Allman. He was always willing to accompany me on my annual summer sojourn to hear the Allman Brothers Band. If you have a copy of their CD, *Brothers and Sisters,* listen to the song, "Jelly Jelly." The moment when Chuck Leavell's piano solo starts will connect you to that part of Joe's soul, joyful as it was, that thrilled to the sound of a flat-out, twelve-bar blues.

I can't leave this topic without mentioning *The Sound of Music.* Joe knew every word to every song. I think part of him believed that there was no problem in the world that couldn't be solved by singing a line from his favorite movie. It certainly made housework easier.

Dance

Joe was a marvelous dancer. On our first real date, October 4, 1980, we went out dancing at the End Up in San Francisco. Joe was wearing a white, gauze, V-neck Indian shirt. He had a full head of thick black hair. He looked just gorgeous. As he started to dance, I was overcome with this wonderful feeling of happiness. I remember thinking something along the lines of, "Oh, my God. Could this be the one?"

I always felt bad that I could not keep up with him on the dance floor. Someone once referred to my style of dancing as that of a Boy Scout marching. I could move my upper body, or my legs, but rarely would the two go in unison. I could go around in circles, though, and every once in a while after dinner Joe would throw on Louis Armstrong's version of "What a Wonderful World" and we would stumble around the living room together.

I am thankful that Michael, Bob, David, Tim, and Vicki could be present today to share their special talents with us. There is no better way to say good-bye to Joe than with music. It is a great gift, beautiful in its own right, but it also reflects back to us the soulfulness and harmony that was at the center of his life.

Cats

You cannot begin to understand Joe without understanding cats. I often felt that he was a feline soul in a human body. Joe conducted whole conversations with Ollie, our oldest cat. I would be in the living room reading the newspaper and thinking, "Who's Joe on the phone with?" or "Did our neighbor Sarah stop by?" No, it was just Joe confiding in Ollie.

Cats, as you know, are great doers of nothing. Joe had this quality, too. He could spend long periods of time just sitting happily in one place.

He had a great need to touch and be touched. He was a deeply sensual person. Again, I felt bad at times. As a New Englander hugging did not come naturally. About six months ago I was on my way to work and gave Joe a one-arm-around-the-shoulder good-bye hug. He grabbed my other arm and clasped it tightly around his back and said, "From now on, when you hug me, hug me like this." I did. Lesson learned.

The cats came in handy here, too. Cats are great touching machines. Joe insisted that we always have two, for the benefit of the cats he said, but I also think it was the minimum number necessary to satisfy his tactile needs. He petted them, groomed them, kissed their paws, held them in his arms, and danced around the apartment with them.

Style

Did anyone ever see Joe when he didn't look great? Even in the morning, stumbling out of the bedroom in his sleeping shorts, his hair pressed to one side, he looked adorable.

He loved a man in a suit. To the very end, he defended Bill Clinton. "Say what you will about him," Joe would say, "but nobody looked better in a suit than Bill Clinton."

Joe wielded a clothes iron with the skill of a sushi chef wielding a knife. The knots of his ties were marvels of sleekness and design. Folding laundry was a profoundly meditative task for him. When he was done he would often issue a great sigh and declare himself at peace.

Our friend Flora wrote me that she remembered walking through an Edward Hopper exhibit with us at the Whitney Museum and watching how intently Joe looked at the paintings. He loved this country's artistic traditions, particularly the Arts and Crafts Movement. His life's dream was to one day own a small bungalow. Knowing what even the smallest bungalows sell for, I always tried to encourage him to cultivate his inner bungalow instead.

He collected art pottery—McCoy, Roseville, Van Briggle. About five years ago on a trip through California he paid what was for us at the time the unprecedented sum of nine hundred dollars for two landscape paintings. We've since acquired many more at antique stores and flea markets across the country. One of his favorites was the still life behind me that I found in Long Beach, California. It was hanging in a store next to an Elvis poster that was selling for fifty dollars. I got the still life for fifteen.

Joe was not an intellectual; he never read criticism. He loved what he loved and his tastes were impeccable. He did not need a book on Mies van der Rohe to know that less is more. He grasped this intuitively. As Flora noted, what was important about Joe was the intensity of his experience of a work of art.

Painting, Hopper, landscapes, pottery, crafts, these are precious gifts, each beautiful in its own right. They tell us something about Joe, too, about how, in his case, style was matched with substance. They reflect back to us the grace with which he lived his life.

America

Joe was born in Hong Kong, of mixed Chinese, German, and Portuguese ancestry. He liked to call himself a mutt. His family moved to

San Francisco when he was ten. He became a citizen at age fifteen. There were times in this country when he was not comfortable. He felt the sting of prejudice and ignorance. But he loved his country. He adored San Francisco—its hills, its lights, its bridges. Golden Gate Park, Seal Rock, Land's End, Haight- Ashbury, Noe Valley.

When we moved to New York in 1984, I felt guilty about separating Joe from his family and his beloved California. He would always reassure me: "This is where I want to live. This is the decision I have made." I know that he came to love the physical landscape of the East and the change of seasons. I know that he came to love New York City, Morningside Heights, Morningside Gardens, the Columbia campus, and St. Paul's Chapel.

Joe had a favorite saying, "Can we take a minute?" We might be on a walk, or sitting on the dock at my parent's cottage, or just watching the late afternoon sun filter into our living room. Joe called these his Zen moments. He wanted to make sure that we knew how lucky we were. He also wanted to imprint the scene on his brain so that the next time he was stuck in traffic on the Van Wyck, or stuffed into a subway car, he could call up the scene and find solace.

Many of Joe's Zen moments took place on benches. It was truly difficult for him to pass by a bench. Nothing pleased him more than to find a tasteful bench in a pretty location and sit and pass a few minutes. I could think of no more fitting tribute to Joe than to find a quiet spot and put a bench there in his honor.

Wilbur Hot Springs, Big Sur, the Russian River, Armstrong Woods, the red rocks of Sedona, the Sonoran Desert, Lake Winnipesaukee, Martha's Vineyard, Central Park, Jones Beach. These are spectacular places, standouts in the physical makeup of our beautiful land. Each is precious in its own right. They tell us something about Joe, too, because he loved them so deeply, stood in awe of them, and studied them so intently. To me now they are sacred spaces, places where I am sure I will encounter Joe's spirit, and places where I hope to scatter his earthly remains.

Flying

Joe loved to fly. As a little boy there were two things he thought about doing with his life. One was teaching, the other was flying. He would gripe and moan about having to put on the old blue dress, as he called his uniform, about early morning sign ins and fourteen-hour workdays, but he never succumbed to cynicism.

He loved his colleagues. Some of you I was privileged enough to get to know—Ed, Bonnie, Craig, Suzie, Juan, Lesley, Kelly. Most of you I have only met briefly or heard about. There was an endless number of stories about my friend Barbara, my friend Tricia, my friend Sarah, my friend Stephanie, my friend Jane, my friend Henri, and on and on. There was an endless number of phone calls as well, and I would overhear him say, "Darling, how are you?" (When it was darling, I knew it was Lesley). "Sweetie, how are you doing? So good to talk to you, hon." I got a little jealous at times. After all, I was supposed to be sweetie, wasn't I?

But there was no point in jealousy; Joe's heart was big enough to take us all in. He belonged to us all.

Many of you know that in 1996 Joe earned a master's degree in social work at Columbia and then worked for a little over a year in an HIV clinic at Elmhurst Hospital. We often talked about his social work experiment. Was it a midlife crisis? Was he trying to compensate for his modest educational background? Did I push him into it? I know at the time that I wanted him to do something more "important" with his life. One of my dumber ideas. What was important was that he do what he loved. We both came to see this and in 1998 he returned to flying full time.

Still, it is clear to me after talking with his colleagues over the last few weeks that he never really stopped being a social worker. You have told me how he listened, took care of you, and consoled you. Whatever his title, Joe was Joe: kind, empathetic, and caring.

I would like to say to his friends and colleagues at American Airlines that you are in my thoughts and prayers constantly. I was honored to be among you on Wednesday for the service of Joe's dear friend Barbara Giannasca. I was struck by the intensity of the bonds between you, and by the dignity and strength with which you honored Barbara.

The depth of your loss is immeasurable, not just because of Joe and Barbara, but because of the loss of the entire crew of Flight 587, and the horrible losses of September 11. I feel confident that I speak for everyone here when I say that we now get it. We recognize that you are on the front lines of our defense. You are part of our uniformed services. Our admiration for your profession and the duties you perform is deep and abiding.

American Airlines is a great company. It is a symbol of our country and a national treasure. I hope and pray that it not only survives, but once again thrives. I will always be proud to call myself part of the American Airlines family.

The Child

A friend wrote, "Seeing Joe's gift with children made me realize that his heart was childlike, true and untainted. There was a quality of life that radiated from him. I only had to meet him for the first time to see that."

Some wise person wrote that while there is very little adult in the child, there is a great deal of the child in the adult. This was particularly true of Joe. He was the most childlike adult I have ever met. I am using childlike in the best sense of the word—full of wonder, questioning, tactile, sensual, spontaneous, joyful.

He adored our eleven nieces and nephews, each of whom he knew from birth. The first thing he would do when any of them came to visit was sit them down in front of the TV and pop in the video, *The Parent Trap*—the Hayley Mills version.

He loved to ask questions. There were times when I got impatient with him, especially if the topic was sports or politics. I could explain to him ten times that Derek Jeter was not a second baseman even though he stood next to second base, nor was he a third baseman, even though he was the third man in the infield starting from first base. It didn't matter. The next time the Yankees were in the World

Series, the question as to why Derek Jeter was called a shortstop would come up. He took great comfort in the act of questioning.

Children are, of course, precious gifts, each unique in his or her way. That Joe was so comfortable in their presence tells us much about him. He was a fully functioning adult, but the little boy he had been was never far from the surface. This was one source of the joy we all felt radiating from him. It also makes his absence all the more difficult to accept. Not only have we lost a partner, brother, uncle, friend, and colleague, it feels like we have lost a child as well.

Sainthood

Joe was no saint, nor would he want to be remembered as such. He need not be enlarged in death beyond what he was in life.

He had his dark moods. He had what he called his evil thoughts. He feared that he would be reincarnated in his next life as the very kind of person about whom he thought ill. He could be obsessive about self-image. I can't begin to estimate the amount of time I spent over the years waiting by the door while he took a few extra minutes in front of the mirror to spruce up. I would tell him that he didn't look any different when he came out than when he had gone in. And this was true. He looked beautiful going in and beautiful coming out.

Once he put on a hat, he refused to take it off in public. He feared the dreaded condition known as hat hair. This is why he could never be a pilot. When we were bird watching on the Saturday before he died and hit a dry spell, he suggested that it was because he had removed his hat and frightened the birds away.

It should come as no surprise that one of the things that angered Joe the most was to be the object of poor service. His own professional standards were so high that it infuriated him to be treated disrespectfully. It was difficult for me to see Joe angry. I didn't want to see him reduced to the level of the people who angered him. I was always trying to suggest a different way of looking at the situation so that he didn't have to be angry. Another one of my dumb ideas. At times he would sit me down and say, "You have to support me in this." Once I saw that the anger wouldn't consume him, wouldn't change him, I would be okay. I could let Joe be angry, and once I let him, he rarely held onto his anger for long.

Joe worked hard at letting go. A lot of his emotional work in the last years of his life was about letting go of things, getting rid of the emotional clutter. Less is more works not just in architecture, but in the world of emotions as well.

I would like to say a few words about our relationship. We met in 1980, and always celebrated October 1 as our anniversary. Since that date we never really parted, although there were times when we were physically separated. On our fifth night together, I asked Joe if he thought it was possible to love someone after just five days. He said he thought it might be. "Then I love you," I told him. Those were also the last words he spoke to me on the morning of November 12.

We were lovers, partners, friends, and soul mates. We had a great run, full of love, caring, tenderness, and happiness. Our last years were our best years. But I don't want to romanticize our relationship any more than I want to romanticize Joe. It isn't necessary. Relationships are hard work. There were times when the differences in our backgrounds and personalities seemed insurmountable. We had our spats and quarrels and unhealthy patterns.

We were in couples counseling for a year and a half, and if it were not for the wise and compassionate guidance of Al Sbordone, we might not have made it. Al showed us that before we could come back together we had to separate ourselves. It was difficult and painful, but I believe that period of counseling renewed our relationship and became the basis of the life commitment we both felt.

Neither Joe nor I were formally religious, although we both thought of ourselves as spiritual persons. I don't know if there is an afterlife; I don't know if Joe is watching from heaven. I don't need to know. For me, it is enough to embrace the mystery of life and to be open to possibilities beyond the reach of my imagination. There was always something mysterious, perhaps even miraculous, about our relationship. We met just weeks before his mother died, as if our meeting was somehow a gift to help ease his pain. We both survived AIDS, although his brother Tony did not. On several occasions early on, when it seemed as if we weren't going to make it, always because of my issues, something would happen that allowed us to try again. To the very end, I was amazed by the strength of the bond between us, and by how fiercely we strove to protect each other.

I am extraordinarily lucky, blessed really, to have had twenty-one years in which I was loved unambiguously by this kind, gentle, handsome, sexy, happy man. I don't think the final chapter has been written. I feel Joe's presence in the room today. Don't you?

WWJD

Al Gore was reported to have had a slogan while in public office that went by the initials WWJD, or What would Jesus do? I'd like to keep the initials, but propose a modification to the slogan—What would Joe do?

I think that first of all he would want us to accept reality, as hard as it is. The reality is that Joe has died, the victim of a tragic accident. He was not at fault, nor is his death the result of a failure on the part of any of us to protect him. He died at his post of duty, having made the decision to continue to do what he loved, fully aware of the risks involved.

He would want us to have our full range of emotions, including anger and rage. He would want us to forgive ourselves for any feelings we have that might cause us to be uncomfortable.

He would want us to cry. "Weep if you must. And weep open and shamelessly before these altars."

He would want us to reach out and care for one another, listening intently to one another and refraining from judgment about the depth or nature of anyone else's pain.

He would want us to become experts in the art of hugging.

He would want us to seek help, professional if necessary, often and repeatedly.

He would want us to use the words "I'm sorry" frequently and sincerely.

He would want us to have our own Zen moments, to find that place, or piece of music, or event that allows us to connect to what is most essential within us. He would want us to treasure these moments, not because they glorify us, but because they humble us and make us aware of how fortunate we are.

He would want us to not just rush onward to the next level or next view or next bird but to stop at the benches along the way. He would want us to listen to the wind and hear in it the "low healing song of time, the hush and sleep murmur of time."

He would want us to work hard at letting go. And at some point, when we are ready, on our own timetable, he would want us to let go of the anger and the pain and sadness and get to laughter. His friend and colleague Juan told me that every conversation he has had about Joe since November 12 started in tears and ended in laughter. To really honor Joe we must finally get to laughter.

Joe had many different laughs. He could be wicked and catty, but his most heartfelt laugh was one of empathy, rooted in our common humanity and shared experience. It was a wise laugh, too, one that recognized that in the face of an often bewildering world, laughter is a vital and life affirming force.

"Sing low, sing high, sing wide. Make your wit a guard and cover. Let your laughter come free like a help and a brace of comfort. The earth laughs, the sun laughs over every wise harvest of man, over man looking toward peace."

So let us think of Joe laughing wisely over every take off and landing, over every workday commute, over every test and every new school grade, over every meal and family gathering, over every stumbling attempt to form relationships, build friendships, raise good children, and tend to the civic affairs of our nation and the world.

Think of Joe laughing with us, and let his laughter be a help and a brace of comfort.

Over Thanksgiving, at my family's house, we spent time going over pictures. I threw away a lot of duplicates and photos of unrecognizable places. My brother-in-law, Rick Howard, whom Joe loved dearly, took two of the duplicate photos and came back the next day and presented me with the framed picture that sits here on the table.

For those of you who can't see it, it is a three dimensional picture of Joe standing in front of the Golden Gate Bridge. Rick made the frame himself, which is no surprise since he is a natural carpenter. What I didn't know is that he is a philosopher and poet as well. On the back he wrote: "Life is a series of bridges. Some are bigger than others. At some point we need to cross them to experience the wonder of the other side."

We have approached that bridge, the biggest one I have ever had to face. Our hearts are broken, our minds and bodies numb, and in the end, words fail us. So, I will yield to Vicki and the soothing words of song, then to prayer and benediction. Following that, Tim Smith will strike up the wedding march from *The Sound of Music* for our postlude. Let's each grab a hand and start down that big bridge.

As we walk we will be comforted by the belief that Joe's earthly cares have been lifted, by the hope that he is at peace, and by the memory that when he walked among us he loved and was loved, fully, deeply, and warmly, by you and by me.

Thank you.

Don Carty Hugged Me

December 13, 2001

Dear Joe,

I hugged Don Carty Monday night. Or, I should say, he hugged me. I would not presume to hug the CEO of American Airlines. We were introduced after the service and shook hands. When he learned we had been together twenty-one years he threw his arms around me and said, "I'm sorry, so sorry." He was sincere; it was a very human moment. I told him that you loved American Airlines. I then pointed to your wings on my jacket pocket and said I would always wear them with pride.

I think both statements are true. Perhaps the first one is a bit sentimental. I know that AA's relationship with its labor force has been contentious and that you were a strong supporter of the union. Still, I remember how proud you were when you got the call to report to training in 1983. It was not just any airline. It was American. I know that after eighteen years you still loved your job and felt that it was the job you were destined to do.

As to the second statement, I am wearing your wings, Sweet Pea, as often as I can. As for *always,* I get into trouble when I start thinking about always. Because right now all I can see is this dark, suffocating pain spreading out forever. It's impossible for me to imagine that I won't think of you every minute of every hour of every day for the rest of my life. People tell me this will change, and I know they are right, but I can't see my way to that day at this point. It feels like if I'm not in pain, then I have abandoned you. I've let you die all over again. Even if I do manage to think of something else for a brief moment, I suffer a kind of emotional whiplash when I return to reality. It's like I've just learned of your death all over again. A part of me dies again.

These last few days have been particularly hard. You would have turned forty-six on December 9. Some of our friends came over to help me paint the hall. I got the color you wanted. I was surprised to learn that our friends are not good painters, nor do they particularly enjoy the process. It wasn't the happy time it used to be when we painted together, and the hall is certainly not up to your standards. I will need to touch it up. But even so, it looks great. You picked a sensational color.

December 10 was Monday, and Mondays are the hardest. I try to distract myself so that I am not thinking about the exact time Flight 587 went down or about what it must have been like for you those last few minutes. I can only hope that you blacked out, or that if you were conscious you were thinking of how much you were loved in this world. Selfishly, I hope you thought of me. I hope you could see me smiling at you. Or maybe you remembered that conversation we had a few months ago when you were obsessing over wanting to get braces. I said something along the lines of "Braces or no braces, you are the most precious thing in the world to me and I love you more than anything." I'm so glad I got to say those words to you.

You may have been scared out of your wits. That's the hardest thing for me to think about. The only consolation is that the time would have been brief. Our tendency is to want to make you all into heroes. Somebody said at the company service, "During the last moments of Flight 587, I'm sure the flight attendants were all reviewing their emergency evacuation procedures." Maybe you were; maybe you were just terrified. Whether your last moments were heroic in the traditional sense does not matter. You always were, and always will be, a hero to *me*.

The company memorial service was on December 10. It was at a Catholic church in Rockville Centre, Long Island. A huge church, another sea of blue uniforms. It was hard at first for me to hear about the others. I just wanted to hear about you. By the end, I was glad I learned about the other crew members. Each one of them left behind friends and family whose hearts have been ripped out. Each one of them led full lives that were brutally cut short. It's not just about you. You weren't singled out for this special pain. This is a big part of my struggle—to accept that this was a tragic accident. Even if it turns out to be something else, it had nothing to do with you the person, Joe Lopes, nor me. Just because I worried about you all the time, just because I wrote a story about a man who worries that his partner is going to be in a plane crash doesn't mean that I crashed Flight 587, does it?

People tell me I am strong, but now that the services are over and daily life has set in I feel anything but strong. I feel greatly diminished, almost like a freak. I've told people I have a hole in my chest, but it's much worse than that. It's like a big chunk of me has been removed. Take a picture of me and, starting in the middle of my forehead, excise a large chunk of my body in the shape of a crescent. My heart would go, of course, as well as my stomach, my intestines, my genitals, and a large part of my legs. Right now it feels like there's not much of me, and what's left is hurting.

The next day, December 11, was the worst. I woke up wailing. I cried in the shower and then again when I walked back into the room. It's so hard to look at the empty bed, where you used to lie sleeping when I came back to dress. (I always loved that moment when I came to kiss you good-bye. I would bend down and put my head into the space between your head and shoulder and you would stir awake and throw your arms around me. Then the mumbled words, "Bye, Sweet Pea. See you tonight. I love you." I would kiss you on the cheek—the morning breath kiss. Sometimes you went right back to sleep. Other times you rolled over on to your side and watched me as I walked out of the room.) I looked into the mirror and cried. God, we look funny when we cry. At least I do. My face all bunched up, quivering, wet, the mouth hanging open, the eyes fearful, terror-struck, pleading for something that can't be. I sobbed all the way through my morning talk with you. I held it together on the subway and waited until I could close the door of my office before I cried again. (I don't bother to keep Kleenex in the office. I just keep a gym towel hanging on the back of the door.)

The news was dominated by the three-month anniversary of September 11, as it should be. I don't know if this contributed to the pain or not. Maybe it's just that it's finally sinking in that you are gone, really, truly gone. People tell me that you are here in spirit and that you are taking care of me or looking down on me. I know they are sincere. But I want *you*. I want your body. I want to hold you and bite the end of your nose and the bottom of your earlobe. I want to fit my mouth around that big, wide chin of yours and feel the rough edges of your whiskers at the corners of my mouth. I want to smell you. I want to slip my hand under your T-shirt and jiggle your love handles. I want your physical presence in our home, where it belongs, where it fits so naturally. I want to hear a "Hey Willy?" from the living room. God, I'd even gladly lay awake all night and listen to you snore.

On the morning of the twelfth, I had a wonderful dream just before I woke up. It started on a train. I looked over and there was Ollie, sitting peacefully on the train floor. I took Ollie to be a symbol for you, and the fact that he was peaceful meant that you, too, were at peace in whatever journey you are on now. Then the dream switched to our kitchen. I must have heard about a plane crash, because I was desperately looking for your schedule to make sure that you weren't on the plane. I looked up and you were standing a few feet away from me. You smiled and said, "Hello." You moved toward me, but before we could hug you melted away, or I woke up. I wished we could have had that hug, but I still felt good about the dream. It told me that you were available to me.

So it was December 12, one month from the day of your death. I was calm. I managed to be commuting between 9 and 9:30 a.m. so I wasn't able to watch the clock. I stayed calm all morning and John Cain brought lunch over and we ate in my office. As we talked, I noticed two all-white pigeons fluttering around outside the window. They are doves, really, as you know—rock doves. I can't recall ever seeing all-white rock doves before, certainly not as clean and beautiful as these two. John saw them as well, so I know I wasn't hallucinating. (What's going on with birds? Are you coming to me through them? There was the extraordinary appearance of the red-tailed hawk in the tree outside our building, the calliope hummingbirds, Rosemary and Elliott's seven-hundredth life bird on the day of your service, and now these two white doves on the one-month anniversary.)

Later that night, my friend Char took me to see the Alvin Ailey Dance Company. There were two numbers I hadn't seen before, and then "Revelations." It's been so long since I've seen it and it was thrilling. Afterward, I entered the apartment calmly and went to sleep. I had made it through December 12.

I had another dream this morning. A man was showing me around a large building that was undergoing renovation and I discovered some of our things in a corner. The man said the building used to be a storage facility. This triggered a memory that you and I stored things there, in the exact spot where they now were. I went running out and called for you. You came over and I told you what I had learned. We went back in and looked through things. There were two very large green watermelons. While I rummaged around you were bouncing a tennis ball off a racket.

I like the fact that in the dream you were hitting a tennis ball while I was looking through our stuff. This is how I would like to think of our situation now. You're off, not exactly at play, but on some very different kind of journey where earthly concerns don't bother you. I'm still here and my job is to rummage through our past and try to make sense of it and rebuild my life. I particularly love those two big, phallic, fertile watermelons sitting on the floor.

There was a sad story in the news this morning. A woman whose husband died in the World Trade Center committed suicide. She lost her will to live, her friends say. She wanted to be with her husband. There were some spooky similarities between her situation and mine. Her husband was forty-six. They had been together twenty-one years. His service was also on December 1. I certainly understand the desire to be together. As for the will to live, I know how quickly that can evaporate. But I am in no danger of taking my own life. I have much work to do. I have to grieve this terrible loss. I have to understand it as best I can. I have to see what life looks like on the other side of this intense grief. I have to honor you and your beautiful life.

Dear boy, do you have any idea of the impact you had in your too-short stay on this earth? Stephanie got it right in her remarks at your service: "Although he had a gentle demeanor his presence was *thunderous,* larger than life." Thunderous, indeed. Someone wrote in one of the cards I received, "The first time I met Joe I could see that the light of God shone in him." Something was shining. We all saw it. We were all drawn to it.

To honor you I have to keep living, and keep writing. Why you? Why now? How could you survive September 11 and then have this happen? How could American Airlines lose three planes within a two-month period? Why has your family had to endure the loss of its mother and two gay sons? Why you instead of me? I know that I will never fully answer any of these questions. I will turn them over in my mind as long as I live. I will write about them and, in turn, create a story that feels true to you, to our life together, and to this season of grief we are all enduring.

It's time to end this letter. I face the same problem I do every time I sit down to talk with you now. I light your candle, then I have to blow it out. I hold your picture, then I have to put it down. I say hello, then I have to say good-bye all over again. Before I can say good-bye I have to try one more time to let you know how much I love you and how deeply I miss you. All of which I'm sure you knew and, I hope, still know in some way.

This time, Joe, I'll just say one thing: Read on.

A Season of Grief

– I –

Two memories from August 2001, a time that now seems from a different era, although it is only four months previous to the time of this writing.

The first takes place at Lake Winnipesaukee in New Hampshire. My family has come here for summer vacations for as long as I can remember. It is a place to which I have deep emotional ties, and my memories are almost all happy ones. In 1985 my parents bought a small cottage on Bear Island, and every summer they graciously clear out for four weeks so that my siblings and I can each have a week there with our families. Joe and I first came in 1986 and have been back many times.

This year Joe's sister Lorraine and her family have flown out to join us for our last three days. On the same day, our friend John Cain arrives by train and bus from New York. Zoe, our twelve-year-old niece, declares immediately that she has a bug phobia. This is not a good sign on a wooded island. Maddy, the four-year-old, has no inhibitions. With a voice that can be heard back at the boat dock a half mile away, she plunges into island life.

It's hard to imagine a brother and sister being closer than Joe and Lorraine. They affectionately call each other Puss. They are much alike, which is a source of their bond, and sometimes of conflict. On the second day a problem arises. I've arranged for us to visit with family friends who have a cottage with a long, sandy beach. They have two girls and an Australian shepherd, the same kind of dog Zoe and Maddy have left behind in Los Angeles. To my surprise, Lorraine declares that she doesn't want to go. Joe then declares that he won't go either, since Maddy would be too much to handle without her mother.

It's a classic Lopes moment, one that I have come to recognize over the years. "We're going," I declare. "Lorraine and Nick can stay here. We'll take the kids."

"No way," Joe says. "I'm not going to be responsible for Maddy."

"We're going."

We get the kids into their life jackets. "They have a dog just like Felix," I keep telling Maddy. Zoe gets in the boat first. She's with the program, encouraging Maddy to get in and come along. We pull away from the dock. In the excitement, Maddy is not even aware that she's left her mother behind. When we arrive at the dock Buddy the dog is waiting. Maddy screams and hops out of the boat. Between Maddy's frenzy and Buddy's yelps we barely get introductions taken care of.

The next hours are ones of pure joy. Adults and kids are interchangeable. We race up and down the beach. There's a huge inner tube that three or four of us try to balance on at the same time, inevitably failing and falling into the water. Jim Louys starts up his boat, attaching a tube to the back, and the girls take turns being pulled around the cove. I sit in the back of the boat while Zoe rides. She seems to be having fun, her eyes widening as Jim drives in ever-smaller circles, creating a heavy chop that sends her rocking back and forth and hanging on for dear life. Finally she gives the signal to stop. When I ask her how she liked it, she holds up an arm and says, "There's a bug on my arm."

John and Joe each get a turn on the tube and I stay at the beach with the girls. Then it's my turn. I had made the mistake of mentioning that I used to water ski, and our hosts insist that I try it. The fact that I was twelve the last time I tried fails to move them. On the first try, I go right over. On the second, I lurch forward for a few feet before letting go of the rope. By the third attempt, I've gotten used to the pull of the boat. I'm hunched over, swaying back and forth, but, as the boat picks up speed, I manage to straighten up. Once I'm up, it's relatively easy. Each time I pass the beach, I take the handles in my left hand and manage a small wave to Joe and John with my right, arm cocked at a forty-five-degree angle, only my wrist rotating. After three laps, I quit.

Maddy commands most of Joe's time, running him endlessly up and down the beach in the shallow water. Sometimes he pulls her on an inflated rocket. Other times they romp together with Buddy. Watching him, I can see that he has aged visibly in the past few years. His hair is short, to hide the gray. His chest seems shallower, the skin stretched tighter across the sternum. He has grown soft around the middle; when he bends over his belly button flattens out into a straight line between the rolls of flesh. There have been times recently when I wanted him to work a little harder at staying firmer. On this day, none of that matters. The distinction between Joe the adult and Little Joey the child has vanished. This is the Joe I fell in love with, and is the Joe that for this afternoon I am still deeply, romantically in love with.

When we return to the cottage, Lorraine greets us at the dock in a cotton dress, looking rested and radiant. To see Joe's family in my family cottage is an exquisite moment for me. The two families, one based on the West Coast, the other the East, have never met, and despite my efforts, would not meet on this trip. Still, it feels close enough.

Many factors went into making this moment: Lake Winnipesaukee itself, my parents' generosity, the deep bond between Joe and Lorraine, and our long-term friendship with John. I feel Joe's magic at work, too. His happiness is infectious; I'm happy watching him be so happy. Some of the credit falls to me. I was the one who pushed for Lorraine to visit. Left to Joe, it would have remained a fond idea. I was also the one who got us on the boat and down to the Louys' beach. The truth is that Joe and I were a great team. With the golden light of the sun dancing off the lake, kids still in the water, adults sharing drinks on the porch, it's clear that our partnership—the "we" that was hatched somewhat improbably twenty-one years ago in a bathhouse in San Francisco—has worked some magic as well.

The second moment takes place in New York. On August 31 we have tickets to see Etta James at B. B. King's Blues Club on 42nd

Street. Joe has been a big fan for years; I converted in the summer of 2000 when we spent a week on Martha's Vineyard with her *Love's Been Rough on Me* CD playing continually in the car. On the subway ride downtown, our thoughts are momentarily diverted from Etta. A young man and woman enter and stand between us, both hanging on to the vertical pole. From their body language it's obvious that there is sexual energy passing between them. This is confirmed when I glance down and notice a very prominent bulge in the young man's shorts. I look over to Joe, who has a much better view. He's noticed it, too. The young woman seems oblivious. Joe and I try to keep a straight face until we get off the train at 42nd Street.

This encounter only fuels our desire to see Etta, high priestess of sensuality. We are taken to our table and order dinner and a bottle of wine. By the time Etta is helped to the stage, the wine is long gone. I order a second bottle. The next day's review by Jon Pareles in *The New York Times* will describe Etta as a "one-woman fortress holding the wisdom of the blues," her voice encompassing "coy teenager and amorous woman, heartbroken lover and spiteful victim, party girl and desperate addict." When she breaks into "At Last," she has the whole crowd with her, none more devotedly than Joe. His response to her is intense; when he claps, he claps hard, holding his hands up in front of his face, as if he were praying. I love the show, too, but it is hard to separate my enjoyment of the show from the joy of sharing it with Joe. I slip my arm around him. I want to be closer to the physical body from which so much emotion is flowing.

Etta is barely on stage for an hour before she is helped from her chair and escorted off. There will be no encore. We file out slowly, not wanting to let go of the moment. Of the major female vocalists that Joe feels passionately about, only two are alive: Diana Krall and Etta James. We have now seen both in small, intimate settings in New York.

Outside, there's a buzz on 42nd Street. The sidewalk is crowded with moviegoers, tourists, and others caught up in the excitement of the revitalization of Times Square. We walk the half block back to Broadway and catch the uptown train. From the 116th-Street station, the six blocks to our apartment are downhill and pass quickly. Inside our building, we find ourselves alone in the elevator. Joe is in one corner, I'm in the other. As we start our upward ascent, I look over. Flush with the emotions of the evening, I throw myself at him. He is visibly startled—he would die of embarrassment were we to be caught—then he surrenders. We make out passionately until we reach the eighteenth floor. In the apartment, we check in on the cats and turn in.

Despite the late hour, we plunge madly into making love. Like any middle-aged couple, we have had our lovemaking droughts and ruts. But this night there is an unexpected feeling of intensity and freshness. Finally, we collapse in exhaustion. It is rare that we are even awake at this hour. We are laughing and shaking our heads as we kiss each other good night.

Many factors went into making this night: New York City and the energy generated by its revival in the 1990s; Joe's love and knowledge of music, inherited from his mother, nurtured and enhanced by his brother, Tony; I made the arrangements and got the tickets (I could picture Joe, sometime in the middle of September asking, "wasn't Etta going to be in town?"); and, again, our partnership. The passionate end to the evening was a payoff for our having stuck together and our willingness to be open with each other.

At some point, unknown to me, the clock passed midnight. August turned to September. We were still ten days away from the day that would change all of our lives. Who can now think about September 2001 and not think of the eleventh? Joe and I would be spared that day, but I believe that if the attacks had not occurred, there is a good chance that Joe would be alive today. Any number of things might have been different, most important, his schedule for the month and the lineup of the planes on the runway on November 12.

So I would like to think that our wild, wine-and-Etta-enhanced lovemaking took place and actually brought a close to the month of August 2001, the last month of relative innocence, the last block of time when I could stake a claim to such happiness.

– II –

Sometime early in the morning of September 11, Joe slipped into bed beside me. He had worked a two-day London trip that arrived back in New York late in the evening. The fact that he was home when I left the apartment provided whatever level of comfort and sanity I could muster as the day unfolded. Like thousands of New Yorkers, I heard a plane fly low overhead as I sat at my desk at New York University, a mile and a half north of the World Trade Center. A few minutes later I stood at the corner of 12th Street and 5th Avenue, looking at a gaping, smoking hole in the north tower. A crowd had gathered; the atmosphere was almost festive. Something out of the ordinary had occurred. We were witnessing history. My sense of fascination repelled me, even as I walked south to Washington Square Park for a better view. A man claimed that the plane was a Boeing 737. I dismissed him as a loudmouth, the kind of person you always wanted to be wrong. Then a massive explosion ripped out from the facade of the south tower. I heard and felt nothing. It was a completely visual experience. The colors were all wrong. This was a perfect late-summer day, painted in blue, green, white, and the silver of the buildings. Now there was a hideous, raging orange and the gray and black plumes of smoke.

Back at the office, I couldn't get a line out. The phone was eerily silent as I punched in the numbers and waited. When Joe finally called me, it was obvious that he had not heard the news. When I directed him to the TV, his voice was muted; it did not reflect the magnitude of what had happened. It was impossible to absorb this quickly. Before we hung up, I told him to keep calling me because I couldn't get a line out. On his next call, it was sinking in. "This is horrible," he said. I asked him to call my parents and let them know that I was safe.

By the third call, he had caught up. "Bill, come home. Please come home now," he pleaded.

I wanted to tell him that I would, but I couldn't. I had a staff, several of whom lived in the outer boroughs, or Connecticut. They had no way of getting home. One of my staff members had a young cousin who was staying in a downtown NYU dorm. He had run out looking for her. "I'm safer here," I told him. "No subways are running. I would have to walk." This was probably true. It also bought me time. We made arrangements for his next call.

On the radio, announcers were using a word from the 1970s: *hijacked*. They were attaching it to familiar names: American Airlines Flight 11, American 77 from Dulles. When your spouse is a flight crewmember, flight numbers are always bouncing around in your head. They provide comfort. They give you the ability to track the plane on the Internet or over the phone. Although your loved one is thousands of miles away he's linked with this flight number, which is assigned to a plane that is monitored on radar and guided home by air traffic control. When the flight lands, its exact time of arrival is posted for all to see.

Now these numbers represented agents of death, missiles raining down on us, and we didn't know how many more there were. Across the country thousands of airline families were in agony. I did not share directly in that agony, but I was familiar with it. On this day I did not have to invoke that unsavory prayer I had uttered on other occasions when first hearing of an accident. The prayer was always that it not be Joe's plane. Which was another way of saying let it be someone else's plane.

By midafternoon my office was emptying out. I had one last phone conversation with Joe and set out on the five-and-a-half-mile trek home to Northern Manhattan. As I crossed 5th Avenue I looked south for the first time since the towers had fallen. I allowed myself one small comfort. At least Building 7 of the World Trade Center was still standing. In the shadow of the north and south towers, it had been barely noticeable. Now it was the most prominent building on the downtown horizon. I walked west and then north, wanting to steer clear of sites like the Empire State Building. The streets were nearly empty of traffic. At points the sidewalks were clogged with like-minded commuters. Periodically I stopped to call home and report my progress. At 79th Street, approximately mile three and a half, I caught a northbound bus that took me to 122nd Street and Broadway, within a block of our apartment.

Joe was at the door as I opened it. We fell into each other's arms and cried. My tears were of relief, and of general shock and sadness. Joe's were of a more specific nature. He had just received a phone call telling him that his friend Dianne Snyder had been working Flight 11 from Boston, the plane that hit the north tower. They had been in the same training class in 1983 and were initially stationed in Chicago together. Both subsequently transferred to New York. Dianne had eventually married, transferred to Boston, and had two children.

Over the next few hours we took phone calls from around the country. With each call, I stood by the window and looked out over the gardens at the center of our co-op complex and further west to the Palisades of New Jersey. I was struck by the contrast between the beauty of the day and the feelings of horror, shock, and numbness being conveyed over the phone. The contrast was further magnified when I took my binoculars and discovered that a ring-necked pheasant had landed in the gardens and was walking about on the grass. He was a brilliant hue of auburn, blue, green, and red.

I was close to tragedy, but not at the heart of it. I felt fear, anger, and sadness, but I also felt recognized. There was a certain gratification in being at the center of an outpouring of concern. People from other parts of the country would say to me over the next few days, "I wish I was in New York." Joe was in greater pain than I, particularly as thoughts of what Dianne's last minutes had been like began to sink in. The pain was far greater still for untold numbers of families. What was painful for others was sad for me, but also poignant. The overriding fact was that at this moment of maximum need, I still had Joe. Throughout the day, between phone calls, we reconnected physically. We sought each other out and embraced. We held hands as we stared numbly at the television.

At dusk we watched on TV as Building 7 collapsed. The last bargain I had made as I was leaving my office—that at least this remnant of the Trade Center would remain standing—collapsed with it. Later we stood on our eighteenth floor terrace and looked south over the twinkling expanse of Manhattan. We had always joked that when we sold our apartment we would advertise it as having World Trade Center views since on clear nights we could see the red and green lights of the spoke on the north tower. It had been visible above the scaffolding on an unfinished part of the Cathedral of St. John the Divine. The view seemed appropriate for our age, a symbol of the triumph of commerce over traditional religion. Now as we looked south, the church was still encased in scaffolding. Beyond, all we could see was darkness.

The next morning we went for a walk in Riverside Park. The air was still. You could feel the natural world beginning to wind down in anticipation of fall. Overhead the skies were quiet, except for the occasional flyover of a jet fighter. I thought of other fall days that were linked to tragedy. In October 1962, when I was eight, I had practiced running home during the Cuban Missile Crisis. I watched a neighbor struggle with his trombone case, thinking it terribly unfair that I would make it home and that he might die because of the instrument he played. The next year, over the course of a few brilliant days in November, we mourned the death of President Kennedy. In more recent memory there was the 1989 San Francisco earthquake. I remember dropping to my knees and gasping when I turned on the television and saw the partially collapsed Bay Bridge. And the death of Princess Diana on a Labor Day weekend, which deeply affected Joe.

That evening we debated whether to stay in or go out to dinner. It seemed wrong to go out, but if we stayed home we would inevitably turn on the TV. We went across the street to a new restaurant, Max Soha. The crowd was mostly Columbia students. Of the conversations I could overhear, most were about topics other than the attacks. This only fed my sense of guilt about having gone out. Toward the end of the meal, Rosanna, the hostess, stopped by our table. She recognized us as regulars by now. She asked us how we had been impacted by the previous day's events. (This was a new question we were all trying to learn how to ask. It was not *whether* we were impacted, but *how*.) I told her that Joe was a flight attendant for American and that he had lost a friend on Flight 11. She immediately embraced him and offered her condolences. What she said next stunned me. "I am from Kosovo," she said. "I am familiar with this."

We did not go into the particulars of her story that night. It was enough to hear the word *Kosovo* and understand that she may have experienced tragedy far greater than what we had just been through. What was new and abnormal to us was commonplace in other parts of the world. As we left, she embraced us both. Walking across the street, I thought about the scene that had just unfolded. My ancestors—English Protestants—had first arrived here on the Mayflower. Joe, the child of Catholic, Eurasian parents who came here from Hong Kong in 1966, was by now thoroughly Americanized. We were a middle-aged, middle-class, home-owning couple. Our world had just expanded to include a woman who was a recent immigrant from a war-torn, Islamic land. We met as equals, shared in a common grief, embraced, and left feeling a little more hopeful than when we had come in. It was our personal version of the lesson that was seeping into our national consciousness, including at the highest levels of our government: In diversity is strength.

It was September 12, my forty-seventh birthday, a fact that hardly seemed to matter. It would be three days before Joe remembered and gave me my gift. On Friday, I sent out an e-mail. In the final paragraph I wrote, "I am at work this morning for the first time since Tuesday. Joe is at home, as of now he has no trips scheduled. Over the past few days I have at times wished I lived elsewhere and that Joe had a different profession. But we will stay here and he will continue to fly. We ended up here seventeen years ago almost by accident; we both have roots elsewhere. Although I have grown to love this city, part of me has always felt that I was still an outsider. No longer. I am a New Yorker now. To some extent, we all are."

The words were heartfelt and sincere. They were written, though, without any real appreciation for the price we would both pay for carrying through on them.

Dianne Snyder's memorial service was held on Saturday, September 22, in Madison, Connecticut. It was another impossibly brilliant fall day. At the end of the exit ramp from I-95 police officers directed us to a parking lot. As we walked toward a waiting school bus I wanted to take Joe's arm. I wanted everyone to know that I was attached to him, but I was afraid that even that small gesture would unsettle me, so I refrained. He entered the bus first. From the back came screams, "Joey! Joey!" He threw up his arms and ran down the aisle in little baby steps. I felt as if I were following Ricky Martin. There were several female flight attendants in the back. He hugged them all and introduced me.

It was a long, formal, Episcopal service. I tried, and failed, to sing "Amazing Grace" and "America the Beautiful." I hadn't been in church with Joe in a long time, and was startled to see how instinctively his hand flew into action to cross himself at the words "in the name of the Father, the Son, and the Holy Ghost." He chose to take communion; I declined. I watched him walk slowly, pensively back down the aisle.

John Snyder, Dianne's husband, rose to give the final eulogy. He was composed as he described a touching family scene the night before Dianne's last flight. His voice began to waver as he spoke directly to his children, telling them how their mother would live on in them. It was only when he said good-bye to Dianne that he broke down. As I listened to John speak, I though about fantasies I had had in which I eulogized Joe. I would play Horatio to his Hamlet: "Good night, sweet prince; and flights of angels sing thee to thy rest!" I basked in the recognition. Now I could not imagine being able to utter a single word were I to find myself in the same situation. In the newly uncertain world that we faced it was no longer far-fetched that I might be called on to do so.

Joe and I made up new rules for flying in the post–September 11 world. He was to leave me a note with the flight number and destination of each segment of his trip. He was to call me from the plane when it landed if he was in cell phone range. Our good-byes became more prolonged and passionate. Multiple hugs, kisses, professions of love, and wishes for a safe journey were standard before he left the apartment. I would close the door and then reopen it to watch him as he turned the corner into the elevator bay. On his first trip back, Joe had a suspicious encounter with a passenger of Arabic descent. He reported it to the pilot, who asked the agents to run a security check on the passenger. The passenger was allowed to remain on the plane, and the flight went smoothly. On a later flight he found himself alone in the galley and felt a wave of fear as a passenger passed him on the way to the bathroom. He filled the coffeepots with hot water as a protective measure.

Flying had changed. For the flight crews it was nerve-racking, at least on the initial flights. I looked at it differently. Ever since the downing of Pan Am Flight 103 in 1988, I had worried about the possibility of terrorist attacks against a U.S. airline. The security system seemed hopelessly inadequate, and was proved to be so on September 11. Now people were finally paying attention. There were still many points of vulnerability but, with the element of surprise taken away, the system seemed as secure as it had ever been, and getting more secure with each passing day. In October Joe held a two-day San Juan trip. On his first trip after the bombing of Afghanistan began, he called me from the plane before his flight departed from San Juan. I could hear the excitement in his voice. "There's a new security system here," he said. He described the security stations the airlines had set up at the gate for further random checks of passengers. He was beginning to feel better about flying.

The period of late September through early November exists in my memory now in a kind of warm, halcyon glow. There was still a great deal of fear and uncertainty and all around us were reminders of the deep trauma and pain that so many others had suffered. Still, the shock of September 11 was receding. On October 1 Joe and I went out to celebrate our twenty-first anniversary at Chez Ma Tante, a quintessential West Village bistro—cozy, charming, and usually packed with diners. It was empty when we entered, and, two hours later when we left, still empty.

In mid-October we went with our friends Stewart and Michael to Stewart's cabin outside of Woodstock, New York, to celebrate his fiftieth birthday. On the final weekend in October Joe and I flew to Dallas for the wedding of his friend and colleague, Kelly. I knew Kelly as part of the tandem of Lesley and Kelly, great friends of Joe's who had been based at JFK for years and with whom he had shared many adventures in London and Paris. The wedding was a beautiful, simple ceremony, made special by the fact that it was one of Joe's colleagues who was marrying. After so much tragedy, it was good to attend a happy event associated with American Airlines. It was another indication that life was moving on.

The reception was at our hotel. At some point in the evening, someone snapped a picture of Joe. It sits above me now as I write. It is the last known picture of him. It shows a man smiling radiantly, content with life. He is impeccably dressed in a dark suit and blue shirt. He is holding a glass of red wine. His right hand is prominent. It is deeply veined, well proportioned, and beautifully maintained. He was his own manicurist. One of the joys of holding hands with Joe was the object itself. I took great pleasure in rubbing a finger across the perfect surface of his nails. The hands symbolized the man—elegant and graceful. Which made what happened later that evening all the more amusing.

We were leaning against the wall talking, each holding a glass of wine. We had already eaten dinner and had a piece—in my case two—of Lesley's homemade wedding cake. It was the kind of moment I loved. The evening was winding down, we only had to go upstairs to reach our bed, the wine had created a nice buzz, and for the moment we found ourselves alone. Suddenly, I felt a rush of liquid down the front of my suit. I looked down and saw that parts of my shirt, suit jacket, and left pant leg were covered with red. Joe had let his wineglass tip too far forward.

He dashed to find napkins. The situation was hopeless, though. I headed for the elevators. Joe was mortified. He wanted me to change and come back down. I declined; I was tired and we had an early flight. He said he would stay on for a little while longer and then come up. In the elevator, I found myself grinning. I was the one who was always spilling things down my front and wiping stains off my shirts and pants. Not Joe. Not Mr. Smooth. His hands, so trim and elegant, had finally betrayed him.

In the morning we left in the predawn darkness. With a smooth takeoff I settled comfortably into the flight. I was rarely nervous when I flew with Joe. It was not his training that comforted me so much as the fact we were together and whatever happened would happen to both of us. What I feared when either of us flew by himself was the possibility that one of us would be left behind.

In the wake of September 11, American Airlines offered its flight attendants the option to take an unpaid, six-month leave, beginning in November. We discussed the option briefly, but Joe was determined to keep working. In bidding his November schedule, he had one priority: holding as much of the Thanksgiving weekend off as he could. He succeeded and, to his surprise, managed to hold a Paris trip. When he had his schedule he called the trip-trading service he preferred to deal with and asked Brenda to give him a few one-day trips on his free days. Picking up two high-time turnarounds could mean $600 or $700 more in take-home pay. As long as they were during the week, I didn't mind.

Joe arrived home from a Paris trip on Friday, November 9. Normally he would have gone out again on Tuesday. However, Brenda had added a turnaround to his schedule for Monday. He decided to put in for a personal vacation day (PVD) so that he wouldn't have to fly the trip, but would still be paid. He had done this several times since September 11 and his requests had been granted. On Saturday we drove out to Jones Beach. I was hoping to find a dickcissel, a sparrow-like bird that had been reported to have been hanging around the parking lot to the west of Field 6. There was also the possibility of white-winged crossbills. Both would be life birds for me, species that I had never seen before. We walked around the parking lot finding many common house sparrows, but no dickcissels. Imitating the voice on an airport paging system, Joe called out, "Mr. Cissel. Mr. Dick Cissel, report to a white courtesy phone, please."

We gave up on the dickcissel and drove to the Coast Guard station. As I scoured the rocks for shorebirds Joe went into Mary Poppins mode behind me. He sang, "A robin feathering his nest has very little time to rest, while gathering his bits of twine and twig. Though quite intent in his pursuit, he has a merry tune to toot . . ."

We walked farther east, toward Point Lookout. With few birds to look at we switched to identifying the planes flying into Kennedy—a Lufthansa 747, an American 767, a Delta 777. We lingered by the water, enjoying the unseasonably warm weather. Finally, something of interest appeared. A northern harrier, a powerful raptor with a bright white tail patch, materialized in the distance. It came toward us and we followed its flight as it hovered low over the dunes in search of prey.

On Sunday we went downtown to pick out a futon for the back room. On the way we stopped at the Chelsea Flea Market. As we walked in, we were both drawn immediately to two small oil paintings hanging high on the wall. They were landscapes in the California Impressionism tradition, a style of painting we both loved.

"How much?" I asked, trying to appear bored.

"Two-fifty," the seller answered in a thick Russian accent.

"Can we see them?" I asked. He removed them from the wall and handed them over. They held up under closer inspection. They were really quite beautiful. "Will you take two hundred?" I asked. (I was finally learning to bargain.)

"Two twenty-five," he countered. "So that I make a little money."

Joe was left to stand guard while I hurried to the bank.

Things proceed smoothly at the futon shop. Joe made his pitch for the one he liked and I quickly agreed. We picked out fabric and pillows. He paid for it and arranged for a Friday delivery, the day after his return from his next Paris trip.

That night I cooked dinner. Joe's job was to get the hors d'oeurves and wine ready, light the candles, pick out the music, and set the table. He tossed the salad. We didn't need to discuss these matters any more; they were second nature.

Later, Joe retreated to the bedroom to make a phone call. I was sitting at the table when he rounded the corner. He had a look of mild disappointment on his face. "I didn't get my PVD," he said. "I have to fly tomorrow. It's just a turnaround. I'll be home for dinner." He turned in early, setting his alarm for what he called "o'dark hundred." Before he went to bed he wrote out his trip on a piece of paper and hung it on the refrigerator, per our new rules.

There was always a part of me that wished he never had to leave, that had never gotten used to the fact that for Joe going to work meant getting on an airplane. I thought little of it. He had come and gone thousands of times. There was no indication that this trip would be any different. I felt no premonition that, except for a brief encounter in the morning, our life together had ended.

I glanced at the note on the refrigerator before I went to bed. The first line read, FLIGHT 587, 8AM, JFK → SDQ.

– III –

Worrying About Joe: A Brief History

The earliest and most abiding worry was about cancer. It killed his mother at age forty-nine. Joe adored his mother and much of what was endearing about him stemmed from her influences. My fear was that he would follow her path of dying.

Had he died of cancer, his death would have been more typical of the deaths of many gay men of our generation, including his brother, Tony. He would not have suffered lightly the inevitable decline of his body and his appearance. It would have been a long good-bye, and he hated saying good-bye. In one of the few letters of his that I am in possession of, he told Lorraine how hard it was going to be for him to pick up and move from Chicago to New York in 1984:

> I've got many mixed emotions. Deep down inside I am excited because I'm looking forward to living with Bill again, staying put for a while, and NY itself. But girl, I feel like I've said *so* many good-byes in the past year, and you know how I am when it comes to good-byes. So I sat down today and had myself a few cries.

Flying, of course, meant that he and I said little good-byes every few days. But in the early days, the fear of him not returning was minimal for both of us. It was only with the downing of Pan Am Flight 103 and then the Gulf War that I began to seriously consider the possibility of Joe dying in a terrorist attack. He was by then flying international out of JFK, traveling to London, Paris, and several cities in Germany and Switzerland. He loved flying to Europe; I saw only the danger in it. At one point I asked him to consider switching back to domestic flying, but he decided to continue working international.

The actual flight was only one source of my worry. We moved into Manhattan in 1988, at the end of a long upsurge in crime. Some trips required him to leave before dawn, others brought him home late at night. I worried about him walking to and from the car. There were lurid stories in the news about carjackings, so reaching the car did not provide safety either. He had a long drive along the Grand Central Parkway and the Van Wyck Expressway. At the time we had small cars, first a Mazda GLC, then a Honda Civic. It was five-foot, seven-inch, 135-pound Joe in a compact car alone in the dark in the big city. I often had trouble falling back to sleep after he left and would lie awake late at night until he returned. The sound of the key in the door always brought great relief.

When Joe stopped flying and worked as a social worker, my fears for him changed. He was working in an HIV clinic at Elmhurst Hospital in Queens. His clients were poor and often in desperate straits. I worried that one of them might take his frustrations out on Joe. After about a year of his working at Elmhurst the old fear resurfaced—cancer. I could see that he was not happy as a social worker. If he was doing it out of some sense of obligation or, even worse, because he felt that I wanted him to do it, then it might eventually kill him. In one emotional conversation, I said to him, "Do what makes you happy. That's all I care about." Within a few months, he returned to flying.

There was always something maudlin about my feelings. It was as if a certain amount of fear about Joe was necessary for me. At one point, I decided to turn my anxieties into a story. In "Widow's Watch," the protagonist, George, is given a spouse, Ray, who flies for a living. George has all of the fears that I had. One day his fears are crystallized when he sees a bird fly into a window and realizes that Ray is flying at the same moment. He fears that the bird's fate is a portent of Ray's. Not sure what flight Ray is on and when it is due in, he returns to his apartment and waits, setting up a modern-day version of the widow's watch. The story has a happy ending—he finally hears the key in the door.

"Widow's Watch" was published in *The Baltimore Review* in December 2000. By then my fears had eased. Crime had dropped dramatically. We had bought our apartment and had an on-site garage and security staff who knew Joe and looked out for him. Joe read the story and told me he was sorry that I worried about him so much. The way he spoke indicated to me that my fears were largely foreign to him.

I know two things about Joe's activities the morning of November 12. His alarm went off at 4:45 a.m. Second, he passed through Lane 15 of the Triborough Bridge toll plaza at 5:51:56. Three dollars was deducted from his EZ Pass account.

I was sitting at my desk when a colleague appeared in my door. It was about 9:40. "Does Joe work for American?" he asked. I told him yes. "There's been a crash at Kennedy," he said. Remarkably, my colleague's partner had been on the flight behind 587 and witnessed the crash. He had just called from the plane. "He thought it was an incoming plane," my colleague said.

"Joe is flying today," I told him. I checked several Web sites. CNN had a headline saying "American Airlines plane crashes at Kennedy," but there were no further details.

I checked the company Web site, which indicated that Flight 587 had departed at 8:38 a.m. This made me feel better. Still, this was as close as I had ever come—the first time an American Airlines flight from Joe's base had crashed on a day he was working. I got a portable radio and turned it on. This was the same radio through which I had listened to disaster after disaster on September 11. One eyewitness described what he called an incoming 767 going down. This was also reassuring; the AA Web site indicated that Flight 587 was an Airbus. Still, eyewitness accounts were always unreliable.

I was alone now, my colleague had returned to his office. I sat staring at the radio, changing the direction of the antenna for better reception. Except for the antenna, it reminded me of a transistor radio I had had as kid. It didn't seem possible that from this toylike machine I was to learn whether Joe was dead or alive. There were more eyewitness accounts, all supporting the theory of an incoming 767. The announcers kept repeating the same few facts over and over. Then suddenly the local station gave way to the national desk with the kind of silly fanfare used to indicate breaking news. I leaned forward in my chair, my forearms resting on my thighs. I turned to the radio and willed it not to say three particular numbers. It would not obey me. I heard the words, "American Airlines Flight 587."

I screamed a single word: *"No!"*

It remains the truest, most accurate representation of my feelings. Not Joe. Not this sweet, gentle man. Not this continual font of joy and tenderness and laughter. Not my light. Not after all we had been through and built together. Not now. Not in this hideous way.

When I looked up, three of my staff members were standing in the doorway. "My partner was on that plane," I said. With those words I stood up and walked into the world of self-conscious and public grief. I put my staff to work. Each of them got on the phone and called American.

Alone in my office, I pounded the table. I swore. I threw things around. I did this consciously, afraid that if I did not display some kind of anger I would pay for it later. I never considered the possibility of survivors. Joe was dead. I knew this. I had thought about this too often for any other outcome to be possible. My friend Stewart's phone number flashed across my caller ID. I would later learn that he had been desperately calling his cousin who lived in Belle Harbor, the site of the crash. Stewart had called because he thought it was a remote possibility that Joe might be involved. I picked up the phone and said, "Please come down." I asked him to bring Michael.

In my imaginary rehearsals I had always called Lorraine first and hoped that her husband would answer so that I could break the news to him. Their phone number was unlisted, though, so I called Information for the phone number of Joe's oldest brother, Mike, in San Rafael, California. Mike's wife, Fran, answered the phone. I had awakened her. It was now dawning on me that it was Veterans Day, a holiday for many people. I had always wondered how I would find the words to convey this horrible news. The word *dead* stuck in my throat; it seemed so vile. I found that I did not have to use it. I could talk about the plane instead. Planes don't die, they crash.

My voice was weak and wavering. "Fran, it's Bill. Joe's plane has crashed."

There, I had said it. Seven words. I had done all I had to do in terms of my responsibilities to Joe's family. A sequence of events would now be set in motion alerting his father and the four other siblings. Not yet, though. There was only silence on the other end of the phone.

"What?" Fran asked sleepily. "Who is this?"

I took a breath and spoke more clearly. I could feel the realization sinking in on the other end of the phone. I heard her repeat my exact words to Mike. I felt terrible. Surely she would be angry with me, perhaps even blame me, as if I were some anonymous messenger to be confused with the message. But she said, "Oh, Bill. I'm sorry. I'm so sorry."

I asked her to call the others and gave her my work number.

I had no reason to believe that Joe was not on the plane, although there was a remote possibility that he had been switched at the last minute to another flight. After nearly two months of religiously carrying around his schedule, I had left it at home. Now that the word was spreading among his family, I had to make sure I had the flight number right. I called our neighbor, Sarah, who was also home because of the holiday. I first had to break the news to her and then ask her to go to our apartment and retrieve Joe's note. I waited on the phone until she returned. "It says 587," she said.

I would not get an official confirmation from the airline until that evening when Joe's supervisor called me. Before then, I had at least one angry conversation with American during which I accused them of not treating me as a spouse despite their avowed policy of recognition of same-sex relationships. His supervisor informed me that she had called me at home that morning, but did not want to leave a message. She then called Joe's father in San Francisco. Eighty-one years old, alone, and blind, he received the news of the third tragic death in his family. My anger at the airline dissipated as I realized what had happened. Joe, dear, sweet Joe who loved to poke fun at me for my absent-minded lapses, had never updated his emergency contact information to include my work number.

Sarah had already performed one grim task, and I now asked her to perform another: to stay in our apartment and answer the phone. She hesitated, saying she wasn't sure she could, then quickly said, "Yes. Of course I can do that." Like me—like all of us—she was learning on the spot. She went to the apartment and called me back with the names and numbers of the people who had already called. Each name tore at me; it was a list of those nearest and dearest to Joe. I chose first to call Lesley, whom we had just visited two weeks earlier in Dallas. I could hear the fear in her voice when she picked up the phone. When she heard my voice she cried out, her voice rising in panic. "I tried to pull up his record, but it was locked. First I thought that everyone's at Kennedy might be locked, but I was able to pull up others." In telling me this, she provided another confirmation.

I next called my sister Anne. Her husband answered. He would later tell me that they had just learned of the crash, and before the phone rang Anne had said, "Joe has to go back to social work." She took on the task of calling my family.

Stewart and Michael arrived. John Cain, who worked next door, arrived shortly after. I assembled my staff and asked them to help each other out and keep things going. I told them I didn't know when I would be back. Stewart, Michael, and I left. We picked up John, who had gone briefly back to his office, and walked west toward the subway at 7th Avenue. How could I walk? How could other people walk past me, going about their business as if nothing had happened? How could the MetroCard reader blithely accept my card and report back a balance? I felt as if warning bells should have gone off. I had no balance—I was operating with a huge deficit. The subway arrived without fanfare, a Number 2 train, one of the old, soon-to-be-retired Redbirds. We entered and I took a seat. The fact that I was going through the ordinary routines of commuting repulsed me. What did it matter if I sat or stood, if I gripped the pole or leaned against the door?

Word had already spread through the apartment building by the time I reached home. In the lobby two maintenance men offered me their condolences. I entered the apartment and found Sarah standing in the kitchen. The cats approached me as if nothing had changed. Pierre, the building porter, appeared and hugged me. Other neighbors followed. My friends took over answering the phone and the door. As the day wore on, the apartment filled with friends and neighbors. I tried to take people aside and spend a moment with them alone. I tried to find something to say to them that would connect them to Joe. When my sister Wendy arrived with the kids I hugged each of them and said, "Uncle Joe loved you very much."

The words seemed so puny, so completely inadequate to the situation. Yet I said them anyway. I listened to the words others spoke to me, even though I absorbed none of them. They bounced off me like raindrops off a car roof. We had entered the realm of ritual; we all knew instinctively how to participate. I would play my role, or at least that part of me that was visible to others would play its role. The outer shell would function. Inside it was different. This was not September 11. There was no poignancy, no gratitude at being recognized. I was at the center of it now and all I could feel was fear, and a pain so large it threatened to engulf me.

Wendy and my neighbor Curtis would spend the night. I sent everyone else home at eleven o'clock and closed the bedroom door. I was familiar with an empty bed. Part of me could believe Joe was still coming home. Alone in the dark, my mind began to work.

This couldn't have been an accident. I was not thinking of terrorism or sabotage, I was thinking about fate. It was my fault. I had written that damn story. I considered the possibility while I was writing it that I was tempting fate. I remember thinking, what if something did happen? How would I live with myself? Yet, I wrote it, I sent it off to be published, and I rejoiced when it had been accepted, thinking that this would help my writing career along. I copied it and passed it along to friends. Look at me! I'm published!

And what about my fantasies about eulogizing him? Did I really want him to die so that I could be the center of attention? I was about to get my wish. Meanwhile, Joe's body lay broken and burned in a hole in the ground in Queens.

What were the odds of Joe being on a plane that crashed? After two American planes had already crashed this year? When it wasn't even his regular trip? When it was an extra trip he had picked up and then put in for a vacation day? No, this was something more than chance. This was some form of payback. This was a malicious fate taking revenge. I had been aware for some time of a kind of balancing of gain and loss in our relationship. Within a month of our meeting, his mother died. Within two days of our moving into our co-op, his brother Tony was dead. What wasn't clear to me was what gain Joe's death was balancing out.

Or perhaps it was just inevitable. Perhaps it had nothing to do with me and everything to do with Joe. Clichés ran through my mind. Why *do* the good die young? Why *does* tragedy run in families? There was something Kennedy-esque in this. His mom, Tony, and now Joe, all taken so young. Everyone spoke of him as such a kind and gentle soul. Was he just too good for this world?

What had his last moments been like? He had been through bad turbulence before. Did he know that this was something worse? Was he terrified? Did he know he was going to die? Oh, God, please no. He was just doing his job. He went to work, strapped himself into his jump seat, and was getting ready to go down the aisle asking in his airplane Spanish, *"¿Pancakes o huevos?"* That was going to be the big issue of the morning. Instead, he had to confront the ultimate moment. He had just a few seconds in which to prepare himself for the end of his life.

And where was he now? Was he wandering in some dark, cold place? Was he lonely? Could I help him? I would do anything, but what? I felt utterly cut off from him. It was as if an axe had removed a limb in a single, swift blow. He had been severed from me.

Finally, around 4 a.m., I cried. I lay on my bed, clutching the pillow, pounding the mattress, and letting my cries escape uncensored. Curtis came and sat with me. When it was over, I felt no relief. There had been no catharsis. Joe was still dead. I was still alone. I hated the fact that I had to face this intense emotional pain. Yet, there was no place to go. For the foreseeable future, grief was to be my full-time job.

Slowly, through the blinds, I detected light. I would later come to appreciate the natural world's absolute indifference to my suffering and its adherence to its patterns and schedules, but on this morning, the sun's rising felt like a personal affront. Without having slept, I showered, dressed, and walked into the kitchen. Curtis sat up sleepily in a pile of blankets on the couch. I joined him. Wendy emerged from the back room and sat beside me. I leaned over and kissed her on the cheek. "I love you," I told her for the first time in my life.

Unlike the Lopes family, the Valentines died in order. Grandparents went first. My parents and siblings were alive and healthy. We had never been through a divorce or separation, never mind a death. We would have to make it up as we went along. There would be two other firsts that morning. One when my father hugged me, and a second when I found my mother in tears as we greeted each other. Joe's love had always pushed me in new directions, expanding the boundaries of my capacity to feel and express emotion. In death, it continued to do so.

From the beginning I tried to prepare myself for the possibility that Joe's body would never be recovered. Both members of my CARE Team—two American Airlines employees assigned to help me—were optimistic, though. They thought there was a good chance that Joe's body would be one of the first recovered and identified. This was because of the nature of the seat the flight crews sat in and the harnesses that held them. In the meantime we filled out a form for the Medical Examiner's office. It was standard stuff, height, weight, skin, hair, and eye color. I was also asked to collect DNA samples. A hairbrush, toothbrush, hair samples from the drain in the shower, and "soiled undergarments" were suggested. My friend Dwight got the first three. I held the line on the underwear. "Was it really necessary?" I asked one of my CARE Team members. He thought for a minute before telling me that it was best to give them as much as possible.

I took the bag containing the other items and went into the bedroom. I searched through the size 30 Hanes briefs in the clothes hamper, selecting a pair with visible skid marks. (Sorry, darling.) I could not do so without thinking of how great Joe looked in his briefs. Now this piece of white cotton—so sensual and erotic in another context—potentially held the key to whether or not Joe's body would be identified. I kissed his underpants and stuffed them in the bag.

The medical examiner's office would notify the police, who would in turn notify me when Joe's body was identified. Word came late on Saturday night. I had already taken a sleeping pill, put in my earplugs, and gone to bed. Dwight, who was staying with me, opened the bedroom door and said, "The police are here."

Two plainclothes detectives in overcoats stood in my living room. One was middle-aged, with slicked-back hair and a prominent scar in his cheek. The other was blond, almost cherubic. They made no effort to greet me. The blond stared at his shoes. The other informed me that the body of Joseph Lopes had been identified. He confirmed my identity. "And your relationship?" he asked warily. "Domestic Partner," I said, sticking to legalities. "Domestic Partner," he repeated and wrote something on the form. He gave me his card and told me I could contact him if there were any problems. They left, the blond never having raised his head to meet my eyes.

I placed seven calls, two to my CARE Team members, then Joe's five siblings: Lorraine, Mike, Rick, John, and Chris. I turned out the light and went to sleep.

All day Monday, one week after his death, we waited for word that Joe's body was ready. Chris Lopes came up from Pennsylvania. At some point that afternoon I caught sight of a large white object in a tree just outside of our building. I grabbed my binoculars and rushed to the terrace. It was a red-tailed hawk. They occasionally flew near our building, but I had never seen one at rest in the gardens. She sat peacefully on the branch. I kept checking back on her. She stayed for perhaps an hour.

From the moment I entered the funeral home, I wanted Joe and myself out as fast as possible. We had both chosen cremation, partly in order to avoid dealing with the death industry. The woman handling Joe's arrangements, though, was unfailingly polite and humane. I had learned a new vocabulary in those few days relating to bodies: viewability and fragmentation. I chose not to ask about either one. I had seen photos of the wreckage of Flight 587. Whatever had happened to Joe had happened after he died. The condition of his body was not a reflection of his character.

We took an elevator to the second floor. At the end of a corridor I caught a glimpse of the casket. It was simple and made from wood. Joe would approve. I entered the room, knelt on the step, threw my arms across the top of the casket, pressed my face to it, and wept. The last time I had been this close to Joe's body was when we kissed on the morning of November 12. Now, I did not know if I would even recognize the body that lay beneath me as Joe. After a while I began to talk to him. I had with me sheets of paper that contained the names of people who had called. I read each name to Joe and told him a little about the conversations. Chris spoke to him as well. I brought Sarah, John, and Curtis up to the casket, identifying them and telling Joe that they were taking good care of me now.

In the morning, we followed a hearse as it made its way across town and through the Lincoln Tunnel. Just on the other side of the tunnel we pulled into the gates of Garden State Crematory. Somewhere, I hoped, Joe was laughing now at the fact that he had ended up here, just outside the Lincoln Tunnel in Jersey, his body being handled by undertakers who could have easily passed for extras on *The Sopranos*.

In the small chapel, I read two Carl Sandburg poems, and notes from Lorraine and my Aunt Rosemary. I asked that the notes, a few photos, and a teddy bear of Joe's be put in the casket. We went downstairs and watched as the casket was moved in front of the crematory. The door opened and it started to roll forward. I reached out and brushed my hand against the shiny wood as it moved away from me.

A few days later, my CARE Team brought me the urn. It was made from wood, the style tasteful. I reached over and kissed it. "Welcome home, honey."

From the moment that Michael and Stewart arrived in my office on November 12, I was surrounded and cared for by a group of friends whom I came to call my guardian angels. I would receive tremendous support from both my family and Joe's, but it was this group of friends—primarily gay men—on whom I depended. They were well schooled in grief and care of the bereaved. For the first week, I called Stewart every morning shortly after getting up. He had lost his long-time partner six years earlier. I couldn't face my day until I spoke with him and heard his gentle words of encouragement. Michael came to the apartment every morning and helped me manage my days. Curtis came at night and slept on the couch. Dwight, a friend who had recently retired and moved to Milwaukee, flew in on Tuesday and devoted full time to helping me. Sarah, just down the hall, was constantly back and forth between our apartments.

One of the things Stewart told me in our morning talks was that it had been his experience that every fear he faced turned out to be human-sized. Each day presented a test of the truth of this statement. I always began my day with *The New York Times*. On Tuesday morning, I asked Wendy and Curtis to collect it from the doormat and hide it so that I would not have to look at it. By the next day, though, I read it. Even when the crew list was published, I looked at it and ran my finger over Joe's name. Laundry also threatened to undo me. I had done my own laundry many times, but this was really Joe's realm. Curtis offered to do the laundry for me and I accepted. When he returned, I wasn't prepared for the sight of wrinkled clothes barely folded and stuffed into pillowcases. I had to retreat to the bedroom to refold my clothes before I could put them away. I couldn't bear to face a pillowcase full of Joe's socks and underwear, so I put it aside. Within a few days, though, I sorted through them, opened one of his drawers in the dresser, and put them away.

The car was the next major hurdle. In 1999, with our Honda Civic in its ninth year of service, Joe capped off a yearlong search by deciding on a Volkswagen Passat. When we purchased one, complete with leather interior, sunroof, and alloy wheels, he declared it our first grown-up car. It was *our* car, but in my mind it was Joe's. I looked on it more as a necessity; weeks, even months, would pass without my driving it. Joe was the Californian, the one who knew and loved cars. He cared for it and kept it clean. Commuting became bearable, even fun, for him because he was in his beloved Passat.

Now it sat in the parking lot at JFK. Two days after the crash my CARE Team picked Dwight up at our apartment and drove out to Kennedy. Dwight drove the Passat back into Manhattan. He parked on Amsterdam Avenue and came up to the apartment to get me. I went back out with him and got in the passenger seat, as I had so many times before with Joe. Dwight drove around the block to the garage and, as was always my job, I pointed the remote clicker at the door to open it. After we had parked, I checked through the car and removed a travel mug from the cup holder. Back in the apartment I opened it up and found it about a third full. I poured Joe's last cup of coffee down the drain.

On Friday, the futon we had bought the day before the crash was delivered. I was out of the apartment and Dwight took care of overseeing its setup. The delivery of the futon was difficult, not just because Joe had bought it and would never see it but also because of what it was replacing. We were finally saying good-bye to a futon that I had bought in 1979 in San Francisco and on which Joe and I had spent our first night together. It had traveled across country with me in 1984, spent time at several of my family members' houses, and finally returned to us in 1995 when we moved into Morningside Gardens. Now it was to go to Wendy's to serve as a guest bed. On Sunday my friend Bob helped me load it into the car and drove me to Connecticut.

The cats were of particular concern to me. Initially the cats were Joe's, but they became mine as well. Loretta was just two and terribly shy. With the apartment full of strangers, she rarely emerged from under the bed. It was Ollie, though, who worried me the most. We had had him for twelve years. He had been diagnosed as diabetic in the summer of 1998. At that time we discussed putting him down, but Joe couldn't bear to lose him. Since then we had administered twice daily insulin shots to him.

With all the activity in the house, it was hard to monitor his eating and get urine samples to check his blood sugar level. One night, I saw he was staggering around the apartment, a telltale sign of hypoglycemia. Luckily my sister-in-law, Heidi, a nurse, was staying with me. Working with Sarah we managed to pump Ollie full of a few syringes worth of Karo syrup, which we kept around the apartment for exactly this purpose. It seemed to stabilize him, and we went to bed. Around 3 a.m. a crashing sound woke me. When I turned on the light, I found that Ollie had fallen off the clothes hamper. He was clearly on his way out. I opened a can of tuna and coated it with Karo syrup. He wolfed it down, and then threw it all back up. After sitting with him for a few more minutes, I went back to bed. In the morning, I opened the bedroom door, uncertain as to what I would find. There was Ollie, sitting in his usual place, hungry for breakfast.

What Stewart told me proved true. Confronting the newspaper, the laundry, the car, the futon, and a cat crisis—each item loaded with history, significance, and therefore, danger—was difficult but manageable. Each episode was human-sized. There always seemed to be a door out on the other side of the pain.

Over the course of the eighteen days between Joe's death and December 1, we put together a service. Every time a need arose, one of my guardian angels stepped forward to fill it. A friend and former colleague at Columbia University offered to arrange for St. Paul's Chapel on the Columbia campus as well as a place for the reception and parking. Michael set about working his network of musical contacts. We quickly had an organist, a cello player, and a singer. Michael and Bob would also perform a flute-piano duet. Sarah did the artwork for the cover of the program. A friend designed the program. Curtis's partner, Tim, owned a print shop and took on the task of printing. My

CARE Team members made all of the travel and hotel arrangements for Joe's family.

Joe and I had never discussed what kind of service he would want, but I felt confident proceeding. It had to be a reflection of his character and a celebration of his life. Spirituality had a role to play, but the focus had to be Joe, not the dictates of any particular religion. St. Paul's Chapel provided the answer to my needs. It was large enough to hold a good-sized crowd, yet it felt intimate. It was aesthetically beautiful; Joe and I often took guests there on tours of our neighborhood. And it came with Jewelnel Davis, University Chaplain. It was instantly clear that she was the perfect person to preside over Joe's service, all four feet, eleven inches of her. She suggested a service that centered on readings, music, and remembrances. She offered to provide a Call to Celebration and a Benediction. We quickly came to agreement on the basic structure.

On the Wednesday before his service, Joe's family began arriving. The most difficult moment was when Lorraine walked through the door. In the past, the reunion of Joe and Lorraine was always the occasion for great merriment. Now, we retreated to the bedroom, held each other, and cried. We each had our own particular issues, but we were united in grief. We were going to hurt the hardest and the longest. Lorraine sat in on the final meeting of my guardian angels on Thursday night. As the evening was winding down, she said, "It's great to be in a room full of gay men again. Just like old times." Of the many variations of loss resulting from Joe's death, this one struck me as particularly poignant. Her favorite big brothers, as they went about exploring gay San Francisco in the late 1970s and early 1980s, had included her in their world. They brought their friends home to meet her; they took her out dancing. She thought of them as her leading men. Both were gone now.

The sky was a brilliant blue on Saturday, December 1, and the temperature neared sixty degrees as both families left Morningside Gardens for the six-block walk down Amsterdam Avenue to St Paul's. We were close to forty strong. Lorraine and I led the way. My longtime dream of bringing our families together had been realized. I looked over my shoulder and saw members of both families intermin-

gling. It was such a happy sight that I could not get my mind around
the fact that it was all happening because Joe was no longer with us.

Lorraine took my hand as we entered the chapel. When we were
settled, Michael's friends, David and Tim, played an excerpt from a
Chopin cello sonata. I closed my eyes and listened. I heard the music
in a way that I never had before. It was as if my ears were newly
opened. For a brief moment, I had an image of Joe hugging me. I
knew that I was going to be all right.

We came together, in the words of Chaplain Davis, "to celebrate
Joe's life and mourn his passing." The beauty of the chapel, the sea of
blue uniforms, the music, and the funny, heartfelt remembrances
from Joe's friends and family combined to make a beautiful service.
When I began to speak, I knew that I was operating under a power
not totally of my own making. Whether it benefited from an answered prayer, Joe's presence, or adrenaline, the voice that came from
within me was in some way a gift. I spoke last, and it was my responsi-
bility to speak the longest. I was the one, after all, who had fantasized
about this very moment. I was beginning to forgive myself for these
fantasies. They did not mean that I wanted Joe to die. They did mean
that if I were ever to confront this tragedy, I would have the opportunity to write and speak from the deepest wells of my heart. As the one
who knew him best, it was my privilege to tell the world what a beautiful man Joe Lopes was. It was my honor to speak openly of how two
men came to devote themselves to each other and how Joe, in his gentle and determined way, taught me to love in a way that I never
imagined possible.

Several miles north of St. Paul's Chapel, at the same time we were
celebrating Joe's life, some of New York's best birders were gathering
in Fort Tryon Park. Two hummingbirds had arrived there several
weeks earlier. At first they were assumed to be juvenile ruby-throated
hummingbirds, the one hummingbird common to the East. No one
paid much attention to them until someone suggested that the birds

might be something else. Any other kind of hummingbird in New York at this time would be extremely rare. Over the course of the weekend the birds were intently studied, and by Sunday a new identification was announced. They were juvenile calliope hummingbirds, a rare western species that nests in Washington and British Columbia. By now these two youngsters should have been well on their way to their wintering grounds in Mexico. Instead they had gone off on their own version of a teenage road trip and landed here. It was the first recorded presence of a calliope in Manhattan.

Several hundred miles farther north and west, on Lake Ontario, my Aunt Rosemary and Uncle Elliott were searching for their seven-hundredth life bird. They were my birding mentors and Joe loved them both. They had booked this trip well in advance and felt an obligation to go through with it. To reach 700 life birds is a remarkable achievement. There were two potential birds that would put them at their goal: an Iceland gull or a purple sandpiper. I told Rosemary before she left on the trip that if she saw one, she could be sure that it was Joe. At noon, the hour when the service was scheduled to start, she left the group and went into the van to pray. I had asked her specifically to pray that I would have the strength to get through my eulogy. As she began, Elliott knocked on the door. "You'd better come out," he said. "The Iceland gull has arrived."

– IV –

December 15, 2001

A package arrives in the mail from Lesley Metz. It contains a framed picture of Joe at Kelly's wedding and a sterling silver bookmark inscribed "Can We Take a Minute?" Christmas cards are arriving as well. They are addressed only to me. This is very painful, like the sudden use of the word "I" instead of "we" when talking about the present or the future, and the use of the past tense when talking about Joe. One card from my cousin Elizabeth is addressed to the cats as Ollie & Loretta Lopes-Valentine. It is so good to see our names together.

December 18

A gray, soggy morning. As I stumble into the living room, I see smoke billowing up to the south. My first thought is that another plane has gone down. Or a bomb, although I did not hear anything. It looks like it is coming from the area just to the east of the Columbia campus. Sitting with Joe, I pray for the strength. When I return to the window, I see two red-tailed hawks circling at eye level. They have been pushed down by the helicopters circling the fire. One lands on the balcony two floors above and remains there, giving me great views.

The fire turns out to be the gift shop at St. John the Divine, an accident. The day proves to be very difficult, with lots of crying. When I get home I find a FedEx package from American Airlines. I recognize these packages now; they contain sympathy cards collected by flight service at JFK. I cry out, "No! I just want Joe." There are cards from the wife of the pilot and the parents of the first officer. They take me back inside Flight 587, where I don't want to be. I feel guilty that I have not reached out to the families of the other crew members.

I have a late supper with Michael. I'm in bad shape; fear is encircling me. Michael keeps reassuring me that it is fatigue. I slept poorly the night before. I go home, unplug the phone, take a Klonopin, and crawl into bed by ten. I sleep until six, wake up briefly, and then go back to sleep until almost eight.

I'm awakened by a dream in which I'm getting married to my brother-in-law, Rick Howard. In the dream he had dated but never married my sister. We are at a lovely castlelike building. I'm having a hard time matching up all the pieces of my wardrobe. My jacket doesn't match the pants. I'm wearing five shirts, all of which have to come off. The bow tie is a very complicated mechanism. Finally, I finish. I'm an hour late. I go downstairs and everyone is enjoying themselves. They don't seem to have minded waiting at all. I notice a group of young gay men parading around, all in top hats and tails. One has red hair and freckles, like I had as a kid.

I wake up laughing. This is the third dream I have had in a week. All three took place just before I woke up and were sharp and vivid, so that I could remember them. The first, with Ollie on the train, seemed to be saying that Joe was okay. The second repeated that theme, but also spoke to my current situation. Joe is off doing what he has to do, and my job is to be here on earth rummaging through our stuff and sorting it out. This new dream seems to be a direct response to my fears of the previous evening. One message is don't go looking for Joe again. You'll never find him. You can have love and intimacy, but not with Joe. Another is that I will get through this ordeal. And finally, people will wait for me. No one is going to desert me because I am in pain.

December 20

I'm deleting some e-mail addresses from my address book at work and I get to Joe. I can't delete it.

Under the subject heading, Holiday Forecast, I send out an e-mail to my family:

Dear All,

The forecast calls for volatility, possible storms, strong lows, and damp-ness. I'm talking about my internal forecast; I have no idea what the weather outside will be like.

This will be my first Christmas season without Joe since 1979. (In case you can't remember, Jimmy Carter was president and Wendy was in high school.) I'm going to do my best to enjoy myself, but I thought I would share with you three needs that I have.

I need to sleep. Please don't wake me up if by some miracle I should still be asleep at the start of the festivities on Christmas morning. I will have my earplugs in.

I need time by myself. Katie has graciously offered me her room and don't be worried if I retreat there and close the door.

I need to talk about Joe. Not all the time, but it helps me to hear stories about him and share my own. It may look like it is difficult for me to talk about him, as I quite often cry when I do, but in the long run it is better.

I will have my friend's phone numbers as well as those of Joe's family with me. I will also have my laptop so that I can keep writing. I will go out bird watching. I think that all of these things will help keep my spirits up. I look forward to seeing you all in a few days.

December 21

An excerpt from an e-mail from my brother-in-law, Gene:

Katie said to me last night that she had cleaned her room up very care-fully because she thought you might need some "alone time" in there dur-ing the holiday time. She wants you to feel that this is "your room" throughout the holiday—that is provided she can periodically enter to add yet another picture of Ben Affleck or Josh Hartnett to her growing array of images!!!!

Things of Joe's I can wear: hats, socks, jackets. Things I cannot: un-derwear, shirts, pants. His closet looms over me. What will I do with all of his clothes? I might have to ask Lorraine to help me. As gay men, we come out of the metaphorical closet to reveal our inner es-sence. Now I will have to go back into his actual closet to remove his clothes, the presentation layer.

December 22

Since moving to New York in 1984, Joe and I celebrated Christmas with my family, initially at my parents' house, then at Anne's, north of Boston. Before leaving, we would have our own private celebration where we exchanged gifts with each other. There's none of that this year. No wrapping, no exclamations of surprise that presents are laying around, no shaking of the boxes, no pretending to be unable to wait until Christmas to open them. I had already bought two CDs for Joe, a new Eva Cassidy and one by Etta Jones, a singer whose music I recently heard on NPR. I decide to keep them for myself. In one of Joe's drawers I discover a present he had already bought for me. It's a field guide to the birds of Puerto Rico. We had booked an eight-day trip there for February.

It hurts to have these gifts and not be able to exchange them. Joe was a great gift receiver, opening every package with childlike enthusiasm. He would thank me profusely and kiss me. He would do so even with gifts that I later noticed went unused. It was more complicated for me to receive presents, although over the years I loosened up about this. One of the many things Joe taught me was to learn to accept gifts graciously.

Sarah has agreed to drive with me to Boston, where her sister lives, so that I don't have to face the long drive alone. On the drive up, I get a chance to learn more about her life. We had been neighbors for six years now but only in the past two years had we begun to move beyond hallway chitchat and cat stories. She grew up in Ann Arbor where her father was a professor, and in Traverse City, Michigan, where her family maintained an orchard. She came east to go to college and spent a semester at Smith College, which she remembers mostly for the fact that Julie Nixon was a classmate of hers and showed up late for class trailed by Secret Service agents. She dropped out and returned to Michigan, living as a hippie and slowly finishing college. She came to New York in 1984 and worked as a jewelry engraver and illustrator and finally ended up in the school system, where she became a substitute art teacher, working toward a permanent appointment. This already qualifies her for sainthood in my book, never mind the steady support she has given me since November 12. She has sat with me through some of my worst moments, and I don't have to try and make it otherwise for her.

The drive passes quickly, and we're soon in Brookline, where her sister lives. She gives me a big hug to send me on my way. I don't even make it down the block before I have to pull over. I can only go so long before I have to stop and let the pain out. Getting to know Sarah better and meeting her family are good things, but hanging over this is the shadow of Joe's loss. I am doing all of this because he is gone.

As I drive north, I feel myself weakening, perhaps thinking of all the times when Joe and I had driven here. When I reach Manchester, I go right to the beach, so that I can have some time alone before seeing the family. I arrive just as the sun is dropping over the horizon. It's warm enough to walk comfortably in my parka. It's absolutely stunning, a complete and total Joe, can-we-take-a-minute, Zen moment. The dog walkers occupy the right half of the beach, so I turn to the left and find myself alone. That Joe is not with me is more than I can bear. I stumble, half blinded by tears, toward the water. No one can hear me above the surf, so I scream out, "NO! NO! NOT YOU!" I keep walking—crying and wailing—until I reach the end of the cove. I sit down and cry for a few more minutes. Then I raise my binoculars to my eyes and focus in on some ducks just off shore. There's a pair of red-breasted mergansers. In my mind, I'm describing it all to Joe as if he were right beside me. I can see him looking at them through his binoculars and saying in a Three-Stooges-Curly voice, "Hey you, little Mergie." I'm envious of them; they have what I have lost—the gift of easy companionship.

Grief is magnified here. Time rushes on, the waves never stop. They have been washing against this same shore for eons and will continue to do so. That same force that brings life into the world refuses to pause when one life ends. When Joe and I were coming into the world, others were leaving it. The waves pounded on.

Later, after dinner, I hit a rough patch while loading the dishwasher. Doing the dishes together was one of the ways Joe and I found to escape briefly from the holiday madness. I try to do them myself, but find myself overwhelmed by his absence. I flee to Katie's room and close the door. Again, I am crying out, "No! Not you!" It feels like I have to lose him all over again because I am in a new place. My loss feels so comprehensive and universal, but has not yet been made specific to this place.

Joe and I always stayed in Katie's room at Christmas while she moved in with her brother. She had twin beds, which posed two problems. Joe was cold without me to keep him warm; I couldn't roll him over when he snored. We were happy to learn that she got a double bed over the summer. Her father told me that one of the first things she said when it arrived was, "Now Joe and Bill won't have to sleep in twin beds at Christmas." I crawl into the new bed by myself at nine thirty.

December 23

A sunny, cool morning. At Singing Beach I can see large flocks of common eiders floating off the rocks. There are many more, but most of the birds are too far offshore to identify without a scope. Walking back to the car a couple sitting on a bench calls out to me "What did you have out there?" I tell them what I saw. They nod in recognition. "I need a scope," I say. They laugh.

Joe loved to imitate these moments when birders exchange information on their sightings. "Whatcha got? Whatcha got?" he would ask with an impatient, pushy attitude. Back at the car I see my reflection in the window and realize that I am laughing. It starts to change into tears, but I stop myself and decide to continue to laugh. It's not that Joe's going to be any better off by my crying.

Woodstock, Vermont. My cousin Karen moved here from Georgia in the 1980s. She married a local boy—Dan Morgan—and they have built themselves a beautiful house on Dan's parents' property. My Uncle Alden and cousin Susan, a flight attendant for Delta, are also here. This is their first Christmas without their mother and wife—my Aunt Judy—who died of cancer in May. Her death is what brings me here, to be part of a community of grief, to spend time with people who know what I am going through. I'm nervous as I arrive, uncertain as to whether being in a group of grievers will fortify me or push me over the edge. Alden is my father's youngest brother. He called me in tears the night Joe died. "I went to church and told Judy to go find Joe," he said. He has become a role model for me. He is up front and open about his pain and his love for his wife.

Dan is the cook of the family and he puts together a feast. There's plenty of wine going around. Dan says that when he dies he wants someone to read the eulogy I wrote for Joe at his funeral, just substituting the name Dan for Joe. "I'd like to talk with you today about *Dan*." When he says *Dan* he uses the kind of voice you hear on telephone voice response systems. "We were together for *twenty-five* years," he pronounces each number with a different voice. Someone floats the idea that a recording of the eulogy could be sold, changing the name and details, such as the type of pet, to fit the situation. "In order to understand *Fred,* you must understand *parakeets*." We are all laughing very hard at this idea, and it is okay. I can only go so long, though, before rebelling. Soon I want to shout out, "Stop! Stop! We have no right to be laughing. We have no right to have fun." It feels like the only way I can keep Joe close to me, to let him know that I have not forgotten him and still consider his death to be a monstrous act, is for me to be in pain.

Alden has the guest room, where a picture of Judy sits on the bedside table. I'm given an air mattress by the Christmas tree. I put my picture of Joe on the coffee table. When I'm alone, I press it to my heart. After a while I hold the picture up so that I can see him. I kiss him on the lips. Back and forth I go, pressing him against my heart, holding him away so I can see him, pressing him to my lips. Crying, mumbling, telling him about the evening, wishing him a good night, until finally I put him back on the coffee table and turn out the light.

December 24

In the morning I set out to return to Massachusetts for Christmas. As I'm leaving, Alden says to me, "I find that with time the periods of peace come more frequently." He hugs me and says, "I love you."

I stop at a pizza place and buy a sub. If ever there was time to get depressed it's now. Alone in a run-down pizza joint the day before

Christmas with a cold, dreary rain pouring down and a three-hour drive ahead of me. The pain declines the opportunity, however. On NPR a geologist talks about how he believes that the volcanoes underneath Yellowstone will someday erupt and cover most of North America in ash. (And I'm hoping that the universe is hospitable enough to support the reunion of the souls of two gay lovers some forty years hence? Oh, why not?)

Later that night my family gathers in the living room to sing carols. Gene serves as music director and pianist. I am able to sing all of the hymns, except the final one, "Silent Night." I get up and go to the back room to put on a sweater so I can go outside. I don't want to ruin the moment for everyone else. I don't make it out of the family room, though. On the bookcase is a framed picture of Joe and me taken at the lake in August. I abandon all pretense of keeping it together. Jim comes in and puts his arms around me as I cry. Mom comes by and hugs me as well. She doesn't say anything; I don't think she can. A spontaneous hug like this is a new development, one that I'm grateful for.

I do finally make it outside. Taking a walk at night was another way that Joe and I reconnected at Christmas. The stars are brilliant. One of the most common condolence cards I received featured the saying, "Perhaps they are not stars, but rather openings in heaven where the love of our lost ones pours through and shines down upon us to let us know they are happy." It's attributed to an Eskimo legend. My rational mind rejects the idea, but my heart finds the pull of the stars to be irresistible. "Are you up there?" I ask. I tell Joe about the evening's events, including the hug from my mother.

December 25

In the morning I lie in bed while Christmas gets under way. I take the picture of Joe at Kelly's wedding and put it in front of me and reminisce about past Christmases. Our first was in 1980 in San Francisco. I remember giving him a poster of Christopher Atkins in a loincloth from the movie *The Blue Lagoon*. I hope I gave him something else, but I can't remember. I get up and shower. By the time I get downstairs many of the presents are already unwrapped. I sit next to my father and unwrap my presents. For the past fifteen years or so, I have been in charge of Christmas breakfast. I make my traditional Christmas pancake. Anne has remembered to get panettone, which Joe always brought. Jim chips in and makes the eggs.

In the late morning, I go out for two hours of bird watching. At Singing Beach, the flocks of common eiders continue. I also spot a common loon, white-winged scoters, and surf scoters. At Magnolia Beach there are many horned grebes. When I get back to Anne's, I place calls to Lorraine, Joe's dad, and Michael. I'm trying to ignore the news, which is dominated by the shoe bomber and the near miss on American Airlines Flight 63. If Joe were flying now, I would be a mess.

Later in the afternoon I take a glass of wine and go up to my room. I sit on the bed facing the picture of Joe. The sun is filtering through the windows as it sets. I talk very slowly, with long pauses, just saying things that come to my mind.

"I have to say that for the most part I have been peaceful today. And calm. I can't say happy yet. I miss you like crazy, but the pain is not as close today.

"I thank you for that. There wasn't a lot that we didn't say to each other. I could say it all a thousand times over, but I know that you knew that I loved you. And I knew that you loved me. That makes all the difference. I know that I will carry that love with me for the rest of my life. No one can take it away. It is like the air I breathe."

I'm thinking about Stewart's wise observation that loss does not shrink us; we grow to incorporate it, and that every pain he encountered was human-size. This has been my experience as well.

December 26

Back in New York. Dinner at Max Soha. I commiserate with Rosanna, the hostess. She lost her brother just before I lost Joe. We have become partners in grief. She treats me to a glass of wine. I try getting to sleep without any assistance. At 12:45 the phone wakes me up. It's a wrong number. I take a sleeping pill.

December 27

I've found a new way of ending my talks with Joe. Rather than saying "Good-bye," I say "Stay near." I like this.

Checking e-mail that night, my heart jumps. I see one with the subject, My High School Friend Joe. We've finally found Mary Rosinski, the one key person from Joe's past with whom I had not been in contact. In hopes of finding her, Lorraine and I ran an obituary in the San Francisco papers just before Christmas. Some excerpts from her e-mail:

My name is Mary Rosinski and I attended high school with Joe. On December 23rd my dad called me and he was crying. I immediately thought something happened to my mom; I never dreamed something could happen to Joe. He tried to read to me the obituary in the *San Francisco Chronicle* but he couldn't finish it. There was no mistake when I saw it. I have spent the past three days crying, angry and trying desperately to control the flood of memories . . . My mom and my father spent all of Christmas day with me remembering Joe stories, laughing and crying, trying to find comfort in an overwhelming void. My parents loved Joe too. He always stopped by on Christmas when we were in high school to visit with my parents.

And the sense of humor . . . I'll never forget when he turned and looked at me and said out of the blue, "Just what gives with Kim Novak? No talent and big fake eyebrows . . . go figure." It just struck us as hysterical. For some reason, Joe and I got stuck in a Black History class in high school. It was a tad "heated" in the classroom since it was the early 70s when all of a sudden the teacher yelled out, "What about you, Joe Lopes? You're no white boy . . . just what do you think you are?" We laughed about that line for years. It was just so in your face. Well, as you know, Joe was not an in-your-face guy at all.

I feel oddly numb, very lost and sad the world won't continue to meet and know Joe Lopes. He was such a nice guy in a world of very few nice guys. I made the mistake of assuming he would always be there and now I can only wish I could have told him how much he meant to me. When I moved to Arizona I lost contact with Joe but I do remember my last phone conversation with him. He told me that everything was good in his life and he was just where he wanted to be. He told me all about you and your life together in NY. Since 9th grade, Joe had wanted to work for the airlines and he wanted to settle down with a partner he could love for a lifetime. He had both of those things when we last spoke. So thank you, Bill.

I had never met Mary or her parents and it had been over twenty years since she and Joe had seen each other. She was a kind of mythical figure to me, a name that stood as testimony to the deep bonds that Joe forged with people. I knew from the way he spoke of Mary that he would be connected to her for the rest of his life, whether they were in contact or not.

December 28

A particularly hard morning. I read Mary's e-mail to Joe. I'm trying to hang on to her last words: He had both of those things when we last spoke. So thank you, Bill. I am feeling very unworthy this morning. When I am confronted with the strength of people's feelings for Joe, it's easy for me to feel that I did not love him sufficiently, that he deserved better than what I could give him. Mary wishes she could have him back to tell him how much he meant to her. If I could get one message through it would be: You were the best thing that ever happened to me, Joe Lopes.

December 29

After fearing Christmas and looking forward to the downtime afterward, the pain seems worse now than during Christmas.

Stewart: "I remember feeling a combination of jitteriness and lethargy." That's exactly what I'm feeling. Stewart: "That passes."

December 30

On the way to Connecticut to visit my friend Flora, I erupt in anger at Joe. Driving by myself along I-684 I spew out, "Why did you have to pick up that trip? Why couldn't you just fly your regular schedule? You had just gotten a big raise. You had just gotten your retroactive paycheck. Why did you need to pick up trips? We had a plan. I was earning more money now, so I would pay for the improvements to the apartment. Later, when you had paid off your loans, you were going to pay me back, or pay for school for me, or support me while I wrote.

We talked about this time and time again. I kept saying you didn't have to worry about me paying out more now. Why couldn't you just accept this? Was this a stupid *ka-chi* thing, where you couldn't accept my paying for something? Was this like haggling over the check at dinner? Damn it! Look at the price I'm paying!"

I feel better after getting all this out. When I arrive at Flora's, she asks, "How are you?" but doesn't wait for an answer. She offers, "Terrible." "Yes," I say, "terrible." This is why she is such a good friend. I don't have to be anything other than terrible with her.

Late that night, back at home, I sit down with Joe and tell him about my harangue in the car. "We were always pretty honest with each other about our feelings," I say, "so I had to let all that out. I know that you never could have known the price you were going to pay for picking up that trip. I still love you and miss you every bit as much."

Ka-chi, as Joe explained it to me, is a Chinese term for a particular kind of haggling. I saw Joe and his brothers engage in it when it came time to pick up the check at a restaurant. One brother would grab the check; the other would protest and insist that he was going to pick it up. It would go around like this for a while until one reluctantly bowed out. Joe and I divided up our financial responsibilities evenly, although in our early years he had earned more than I did and often paid a greater share of the household expenses. In the past few years I had begun to earn considerably more than Joe. With student and car loans and a mortgage, he could not afford to save any money. I could, and used my savings to pay for renovations to our kitchen in April 2001. I was prepared to pay for more renovations. At some point we would sit down and figure out who owed what to whom. I thought it was a good plan, I thought Joe did too, except periodically he would insist that he had to contribute to the renovations. The only way he could do that would be to fly more hours.

It was only after Joe's death that I began to think about our financial relationship in terms of *ka-chi*. I think it was difficult for him to accept my paying for things. How much it bothered him, I'll never know. Did *ka-chi* kill him? I asked Lorraine this in an e-mail, and she wrote back As far as *ka-chi,* if he only knew that's what killed him he'd probably die laughing. She's right about his reaction, but I think the answer is no. He would have picked up extra trips whether or not I was paying for the renovations. Life costs money. Joe and I both struggled with how much was enough. We wanted things. We wanted to not want things. In the end the routine we both agreed to was that he would pick up a few extra trips a month on weekdays when I was working. It worked fine until he got on a doomed plane. That's what killed him.

January 1, 2002

The new year is finally here. My mantra is, "It can't possibly be worse than the last one."

I was calm last night, all of yesterday, actually, and all of this morning, so far. I went into the bathroom once last night at Stewart's and wept. It's not that something came up and I fled to the bathroom. I went to the bathroom and once I was alone I began to cry. Crying and urinating go hand in hand these days, since it is when I am alone. Again, the word *monstrous* came to mind when I think that Joe has been taken from us, as well as the way in which he was taken. I can only go so long socializing and pretending to be happy without stopping to recognize this fact. After I got home I had a talk with Joe. Yes, I'm glad that the old year is gone, but what joy is there in starting my first year without him?

– V –

No one is certain when the first Lopes arrived in Macao, the small, rocky peninsula on the coast of southern China. Settled by the Portuguese in the sixteenth century, Macao had long since been overshadowed by Hong Kong and was considered a backwater for gambling when Joe's great-grandfather, Constantino José Lopes, moved his family to Hong Kong in the nineteenth century. It was at this point that pronunciation of the family's name became anglicized, changing from *LA pesh* to *Lo pes*. In America it would be both Hispanized and Americanized. Joe opted for the Hispanic *Lo pez* since most people pronounced it that way regardless of the *s* at the end. The popularity of the baseball player Davey Lopes made possible the single-syllable pronunciation, *Lopes*, like *slopes*, which Joe's younger siblings adopted.

Joe's paternal grandfather was born a British subject in Hong Kong. When he found his opportunities limited by Britain's tight control of the economy, he took a job with a British import/export company in the booming international settlement of Shanghai. Joe's father, John, was born there in 1920. His mother, Lily, was also born in Shanghai, ten years later. Her father was a university professor from a well-connected family in Chengdu province. Her mother was a blonde, blue-eyed German who met her future husband in Germany, married him, and agreed to return to China to live with him.

The 1930s and 1940s were decades of turmoil and profound transformation for China. Joe's parents were swept up in multiple national and international dramas. They lived through the Japanese occupation of Shanghai during World War II. They married in 1950, and Joe's eldest brother Michael was born in January 1951. By then Mao had triumphed and the People's Republic of China was established. This posed two problems for the Lopes family. First, John felt threatened because of his Catholicism. Second, Lily's father was an outspoken opponent of Communism. He was quickly imprisoned and would later develop pneumonia in jail and die in 1957 in China.

In 1951 the family was granted permission to leave, going first to Macao, and then Hong Kong, where Joe was born in 1955, Lily and John's fourth son. His Portuguese birth certificate reads José Maria. On the English birth certificate, it was translated as Joseph Mary. Shortly after Joe was born his father applied for permission to immigrate to the United States. Because of strict quotas on the number of Chinese immigrants, it took ten years before his application was approved. In August, 1966, the Lopes family boarded the SS *Cleveland* in Hong Kong. After stops in Japan and Hawaii, they sailed into San Francisco Bay. The kids—there were six now, Lorraine and Rick had been born in 1960—all gathered on the deck in hopes of seeing the Golden Gate Bridge, but it was hidden in the fog.

By the time Joe's family sailed into San Francisco Bay in 1966, each of the roots of my family had been established in North America for generations. My mother was, like Joe, a first-generation immigrant, although she never thought of herself in that way. Her parents moved to Connecticut from Ottawa, Canada, when she was an infant. Her ancestors were Scottish and Irish. My father's family was British and had lived in New England since the arrival of the Mayflower. My heritage was stable, middle-class, and conservative. My elders were churchgoers and Republicans, and saw no contradiction between the two. Families are never what they appear to be on the surface, though, and the Valentines are no exception. The family tree that my grandfather Valentine so painstakingly constructed can only reveal so much. I know there were some prominent "bachelors" in the lineage, but they don't appear on the family tree—only those who procreate make it.

Grandpa's sister, Great-Aunt Ruth, never married. When Joe and I made our first trip from San Francisco to the East Coast in 1982, we picked up Auntie Ruth and drove her to my grandparents for dinner.

Later that night, as we dropped her off at her home she said to me, "I'm so glad you've found such a nice . . ." She searched for a word and then settled on "partner." It was the last time we spoke. Later that year she fell and hit her head and never fully recovered. The next time I saw my grandfather he told me that Auntie had gone in and out of lucidity during her last days, and that once, when he was visiting with her, she had sat up in bed and asked, "Where's Joe the Chinaman?"

The phrase *Chinaman* never failed to elicit a laugh when I told the story. It reveals the provincialism that was certainly a part of Auntie's life. The story as a whole, though, is deeply moving to me, especially in light of her earlier recognition of Joe as my partner. As a young woman Auntie went to California and she told me that if she had stayed there her life would have been very different. Instead, duty and tradition summoned her home. Perhaps she saw in my going to California and finding Joe a reflection of what her life might have been like had she lived in a different time. Perhaps her last words to me were her way of blessing our union.

That my great-aunt, proud descendant of Mayflower settlers and a devout Christian would, as she lay dying, summon the name of my Chinese lover from her subconscious mind is another of the mysteries that surrounds my relationship with Joe. It feeds the sense I have that Joe and I were destined to meet and be together and enter fully into each other's family. A symbol of that destiny has existed for some time now in our kitchen. It is Grammy Valentine's green Depression-glass cookie jar. She kept it stocked with homemade Toll-House cookies and, as a child, I always stopped there when I visited. At some point I inherited it. Since we didn't regularly keep cookies around the house, it became the rice jar. Joe bought rice by the twenty-pound bag, which he kept in the pantry. Periodically he would pull the bag out and refill the cookie jar. In doing so he was not just ensuring that his favorite carbohydrate was close at hand; he was also replenishing the mystery that lay at the heart of our relationship, that sense that our connection ran deeper than the two of us and that our finding each other was more than just luck.

𝒫

Beginning in the seventeenth century, if not earlier, ancestors of the present- day Lopes and Valentine families—Chinese, German, Portuguese, English, Irish, and Scottish—left their homes, crossed continents and oceans, and endured wars, religious strife, and economic hardship to improve their lives and those of their progeny. They were part of the great social movements bringing the modern world into existence. In some cases, forces beyond their control swept them along, such as when the Lopes fled Shanghai following the communist takeover of China. In other cases, individuals acted courageously, such as my Pilgrim ancestors settling in the New World, or Joe's German grandmother (Oma) setting off to China with the man she loved. Even as they participated in transformational events, many remained deeply conservative. They brought their Old World prejudices with them. (My mother's grandfather, Billy Kelly, was virulently anti-Catholic. He once walked out the room when my mother came home with a Catholic date.) Yet, the fact that Joe and I could meet and fall in love and live a relatively open life is in many ways a logical result of our ancestors' actions. They broke down rules that had prohibited people from forming unions across racial and religious lines. The movement for gay liberation, like other movements of the twentieth century, would not have been possible without the legacies bequeathed to us by our ancestors.

The last journey that had to take place before Joe and I could meet was for me to get to San Francisco. It did not seem a likely occurrence. At the time of my birth—midcentury, a middle child in a middle-class family in the middle of a state whose identity was formed largely by the fact that it lay midway between New York and Boston—all things pointed toward the center. I was on track for a life of modest ambitions. As the 1960s unfolded, that began to change. My rebellious instincts were not tamed by the 1970s or by a confrontation with reality after graduating from college. I still needed something more. I was to be the Oma of the Valentine family. In 1978 I packed a trunk, foam mattress, and guitar onto a Greyhound bus, and headed west.

– VI –

Joe's favorite knock-knock joke: Knock knock. Who's there? Sam and Janet. Sam and Janet who? (Sung to the tune of "Some Enchanted Evening") Sam and Janet evening...

When I saw Joe on October 1, 1980, it was not across a crowded room. Nor was he a complete stranger.

We were at the Club Baths in San Francisco. Wednesday night was coupon night, which lowered the price of a locker to $2.00. The line was out the door when I arrived. Joe stood a few people in front of me. By the time I changed and showered I had already made up my mind that I would try to find him.

He was sitting on a bench along a dark hallway on the third floor. Like everyone, he wore only a towel around his waist. In one hand he held a pack of cigarettes, in the other, a bottle of poppers. Overhead, a long-forgotten disco tune was blaring. Such was the raw material out of which enchanted evenings were created in pre-AIDS San Francisco.

I had met Joe briefly eight months earlier. He was dating my roommate and came to our flat for dinner. I remembered his name and that he worked at Macy's. Now I tried to work these facts into an opening line so that I could approach him. Something other than the standard, "Hi. How are you? Do you come here often?" Before I got up the courage to make my move a man approached me. He was a teammate from the softball league I played in. I had no interest in talking with him, which I tried to make clear so that he would move on before Joe did. Rather than taking the hint, he settled in. We were standing in front of a window. It was an unusually warm night and the window had been pushed open from the bottom. My teammate leaned both forearms against the sill and looked outside. Suddenly the window gave way and crashed on his head, shattering a small pane of glass. He stepped back, stunned. He ran off to make sure that he had not been cut.

I had my opening line. I turned to Joe and asked, "Did you see that?" I sat down on the bench next to him. "You're Joe, right? You work at Macy's?" He was surprised that I knew this. He had not remembered me. We talked until Joe offered to buy me a drink downstairs. We drank apple juice out of plastic cups; no liquor was allowed on the premises. Later, we visited the bunkroom. When we had showered and dressed, Joe offered me a ride home. We drove first to Church Street Station for cake and coffee and then to my flat on Laguna Street. Joe Lopes was the only man ever to buy me a drink and give me a ride home from the baths. Now it was my turn to make an offer. As we sat in his red Honda Civic I asked him if he would like to spend the night. He said yes.

The next night, I went out to Joe's and our relationship was unexpectedly baptized. We stopped at Ocean Beach on the way to the house he shared with Lorraine. At one point, as we watched the sun setting on the horizon, a wave rushed past, curved back, and trapped us. Before we could jump out of the way our feet were soaked.

Two nights later we went out dancing. Although I don't remember what song was playing when we took the floor, I will never forget the sight of Joe as he began to dance. He held his arms out to the side; his shoulders, hips, and legs moved effortlessly. They all worked together, flowing seamlessly. He danced with the ease of a curtain caught in a gentle wind. As he came closer to me, he smiled radiantly. It is natural to believe that an outward grace is a reflection of an inner beauty, although reality often proves otherwise. In Joe's case it was true. I had known him for just seventy-two hours and from the beginning I knew that I liked him. It wasn't until I saw him dancing, though, that my feelings began to run deeper.

The next night, lying in his arms in my bed, I told him that I loved him. In retrospect, it seems an extraordinary thing to say to a man whom I had known for only five days. I was certainly not speaking from experience. I was twenty-six, but all my previous expressions of love had gone unrequited. I was used to measuring the depth of my love by the intensity of my pain. This was something new. Joe was not like most of the young men I had pined after since moving to San Francisco. I did not fear that by telling him I loved him I would drive him away. He was accessible. After he died, others would tell me about the light that shone from within him. This is what I saw that night on the dance floor at the End Up. He danced his way into my heart, and my life.

The saying goes that when God closes a door, He opens a window somewhere else. In this case a window came crashing down and a door opened. I may never have met Joe if he hadn't dated my roommate. If my roommate had not broken up with him, Joe's too-short stay on this planet may have been even shorter. My roommate died of AIDS in 1992. Had I not met Joe that night, the opportunity might have been lost for good. My life had taken a dangerous turn. Over the previous year, I had been drawn into a relationship with a group of people who, under the guise of changing the world, had staked an expanding claim to my time, what little money I had, and my conscience. Over the next six months the free time necessary to meet someone and establish a relationship would vanish from my life.

Four weeks after we met, on a sidewalk outside of Holy Name Catholic Church in the Sunset District, Joe held me as I cried in his arms. His mother, Lily Delores Lopes, was dead. I never met her, although I believe that Joe had told her about me. She was forty-nine. In her short life she survived the Japanese invasion of China, fled Shanghai for Hong Kong in the wake of the communist takeover, and moved her family to the United States. In addition to raising seven children and caring for her husband, who was legally blind, she worked full time as a secretary for the Bechtel Corporation. In the month in which I had known Joe, the depth of his love for his mother had been made clear. Yet, I was the one who was crying. Partly it was out of gratitude. In the previous two weeks, as Lily's condition worsened, we had drawn closer. I still could not believe my good fortune at having met Joe and having been accepted into his family. I was also feeling a great deal of sadness. Joe's loss of his mother made me feel the loss of any relationship with my mother. For the time being we were estranged, largely because of what was perceived as my lifestyle choice of moving to San Francisco and being gay. Seeing the depth of the bond between Joe and Lily, I had hoped that she would become a mother figure for me as well. Finally, there was fear. As much as I loved Joe and wanted to be with him, I could not ignore the demands of the other part of my life. I was afraid that I had already given away too much and did not know how to get it back.

– VII –

My first day back at work after the Christmas break. I delete the entry "Joe" from my e-mail address book. It's quick and relatively painless. Eudora does not ask me, "Are you sure you want to delete 'Joe' from your address book?" Or even worse, "Are you sure you want to send 'Joe' to the recycle bin?" I might have backed out then. Instead, it just disappears.

After work I'm off to PETCO to continue my search for the perfect kitty litter solution. This has been going on for almost a year now. It's largely been my search; Joe watched from the sidelines with an attitude of bemusement. The problem is this: Ollie is a diabetic and he produces copious amounts of urine. I'm tired of the smell. I hate the sight of the box itself. I hate the crunch of stray pellets underfoot. I've tried all of the different kinds of litter. Each of them wilted under Ollie's onslaught, and I am back where I started, with clay. I've tried different locations, too—the front closet, the hall, the back bedroom closet.

With this trip to PETCO, the experiment resumes. Leaving the store, I feel ecstatic. I've discovered the Booda Dome! It is the same concept of the Booda Box in that it is covered, but it is in the shape of a dome. It's very stylish and will take up considerably less space than the Booda Box. I take note of the dimensions so that I can go home to measure Ollie to make sure that he fits.

After PETCO I stop at Barnes & Noble to buy C. S. Lewis's *A Grief Observed*. My feeling of happiness lingers through this transaction, and as I walk across 18th Street to the subway I feel as if I am practically floating. It's a strange happiness and I don't trust it. It's not connected to Joe, and for so many years happiness had been connected to him. I feel the need to get home quickly and talk to Joe to see if this happiness can be connected to him. But I can't be connected if I'm happy, right? Can't I only be connected to him when I am sad?

I measure Ollie. He will fit in the Booda Dome.

January 3

My first solo laundry experience since November 12. The laundry room is empty and it goes well until I pull the clothes out of the second washer. All my whites are now yellow. What did I do wrong? I know that I could bleach them, but this is something I have never done. It's just underwear and one T-shirt, so I throw it all away.

January 4

E-mail from Mary Rosinski:

One of Joe's favorite expressions in high school was "He's the kind of guy that can lift a ton but can't spell it." It never failed to make me laugh. He had a navy blue scarf that was about 6 feet long . . . it went on and on. And I remember once admiring it and Joe took it off and gave it to me. Where are those things now? Please remember that in your relationship with Joe you compromised, you gave things up for the sake of the relationship, you got hurt and you had to let go. Don't forget that. And you will love again some day, Bill, but it will be different because you will be different. That's not a betrayal—that's a gift that Joe left.

January 5

A scene in the elevator as I'm leaving the building: a neighbor and her daughter get on at the fourteenth floor. Anne is French.

"Hello Bill! Are you going to the gym?"

"No, the post office."

"Oh! Too bad. I hate that post office."

At the next stop, a young black man—whom I've always assumed is gay—gets on with his laundry. At the third stop, a middle-aged black man with a beret gets on. He's obviously friends with Anne.

"Hello, mademoiselle!"

"Oh, please! Mademoiselle?"

He points to her daughter. "Mademoiselle?"

"Yes, she is mademoiselle."

He points to the young man with the laundry. "Mademoiselle?"

He replies, "Oh, no. 'Monsieur.'"

We all laugh. It's a lovely Morningside Gardens scene and as it unfolds my eyes are a camera, relaying it all to Joe. It is something that I would have taken great pleasure in describing to him. Can I enjoy the scene just for myself, just because it makes me happy, not because it would make Joe happy and the making of Joe happy would in turn make me happy?

Recent junk mail for Joe: A flyer for a conference: "Narcissism Revisited." A flyer from Social Circles: "Enhance Your Social Life with the Activity and Social Club for Successful New Yorkers." Twenty years from now, will junk mail still be arriving for Joe? How long does junk mail outlive us?

I'm amazed at how much bargaining you can do after death. Every time I see a pre-November 12 date, I can't help but ask, can't we go back to that date? If the date is between 9/11 and 11/12, I feel guilty. How could I just ask to go back that far, were I suddenly granted this power to roll back the calendar. Wouldn't I have to go all the way back to 9/10?

January 6

Things Joe just missed: New floors in the elevators, repaving 125th Street, Listerine PocketPaks.

At home, I cook my first real dinner, the kind I would have cooked for the two of us—salmon, sautéed spinach, stewed white beans. Chocolate sorbet for desert. I even go so far as to have a small glass of Scotch with it. I don't eat at the table, but on the couch. I put Joe's candle and picture on the coffee table. I clink my glass against the picture frame. Later, I call Michael to record the milestone.

January 7

On the train this morning I think about forgiveness and how vital it is to relationships. We wish our partners to be perfect, but they can't be. There was much I needed to be forgiven for, and Joe did. What about now? Can I forgive him for leaving me? For picking up this trip that he didn't have to pick up? Can you forgive the dead?

It's Monday morning. Rather than sit and watch the clock tick down to 9:17, the time of death according to the death certificate, I go out and mail two letters. I know enough time has not passed, so I walk over to PETCO. I purchase the Booda Dome and their special clumping litter. If Joe is watching, he is surely smiling now.

At dinner with Joe's colleague, Juan Ortega, I ask him, "Isn't there any dirt you can tell me about Joe? Was he always as nice and kind as everyone says?" Juan replies, "Sorry, I'm afraid that he was. The only thing I can think of is that trip when the cast of the all-male *Swan Lake* was on the plane. Every time one of them got up, Joe was in the aisle to check him out."

Juan talks about how angry he was when his lover John died. The world just goes on. I get angry when I see young couples, too. I want to run up to them and warn them, Don't do it! You don't know when or how it will end. It's too painful!

More than young people, I'm having a hard time with old people. I'm afraid of them now. I had this nice idea of Joe and I growing old together at Morningside Gardens. Now, I fear I will be like one old man who lives in our building—disheveled, unkempt, his shoes falling apart, food stains on his shirt, farting in the elevator.

Sarah comes over with news. She has been appointed art teacher at the elementary school across the street. We have a drink. It's the second day in a row I have been able to have a glass of Scotch. Joe would be so proud of Sarah's achievement.

The Booda Dome is brought home and set up. At the end of the night, I put litter in it, keeping the old box full as well. In the morning, I find a present from Ollie. Oh joy!

– VIII –

January 10

Dinner with Dwight, Ben, and Michael. It is hard to be in their apartment and see Ben, who is Korean. I hold on to him for a long time when he hugs me. When I get home, I fly into a rage, pounding pillows on the couch, throwing my clothes all over the room as I undress. No good-night talk with Joe. I look at the picture of us on the dresser. Why did you leave me? Why?

There is urine on the liner on the closet floor. A flaw in the Booda Dome: What is to stop Ollie from facing inward and peeing out the opening onto the floor?

I take a pill and crawl into bed.

January 11

I wake up on Joe's side of the bed for the first time. It feels good. An e-mail to Michael:

What struck me was the realization that Joe and I are in different places now, physically and emotionally, and that I don't have him to help me through this. He would have been so good at helping me, just as I helped him through the loss of Lily, Tony, and Dianne. This is my first big loss and the one person I need the most is not here to help me through it. In life, it always bothered me when we were out of synch and what we were so good at is eventually finding common ground, or at least being clear on what our differences were. How do we do that now? Or don't we? Do I have to let him go? That's what kills me.

Michael's response:

Regarding finding the balance again with Joe, all I can say is that I believe you will. Having conversations with him as you already do, I feel that little by little you will regain some sort of communication with him. It will be different, of course, but my heart tells me that a way will be found for you to continue your lifeline to one another. Just keep up the talks and I think Joe will let himself be heard to you.

What I miss most of all today: The way he would walk up to me while I was cooking or doing the dishes and put his hands around my upper arm and press his nose into my shoulder or neck. The way he would hang on to me. Sometimes it bothered me, like he was literally hanging on to me too much, but mostly it was lovely. Just another of the many ways in which we were in physical contact.

January 12

The second month anniversary. I busy myself around nine o'clock, and sit down with Joe around nine twenty, the time of death safely behind me. I read to him from my writing. I talk more with him about the fact that we are in such different places now, and about the pain I feel that he is not here to help me through my first big loss. This is the bargain we accept though, when we enter relationships. We don't think too much about it. It would drive us crazy if we did. We give ourselves to someone else, aware that one of us is going to die first and we have no way of knowing who it will be and how long before the other one goes. What a crazy deal that is. Shouldn't we negotiate better terms? Shouldn't we at least be guaranteed a certain window of time together and a reasonable shot at going roughly around the same time so no one is left facing such a long stretch of grief?

I can't get my head around the idea that I may live another forty or fifty years and that for every second of that time Joe will not be here. It's not difficult envisioning being sexually active, but loving someone else? Sharing a home with someone else? Lying in bed with another man, gently biting his ear, listening to his heart beat, and telling him I love him? And at the same time thinking that Joe would want me to be doing this? Joe is up there rooting for me? The thought of it almost makes me physically ill. And what will allow me to do this? The passage of time? What does time change? And yet what is the alternative, the rest of my life without the kind of intimacy that Joe and I had, and which I so treasured?

This is what makes me feel that at some point I have to let Joe go, cut him off, and this is what I cannot fathom. But hasn't death already done that? Hasn't death taken him, cut him off, at least physically, from me? How do I stay connected with him and still have a life of my own?

Maybe I need to cut myself some slack on this. Maybe I don't need to figure this out now. Maybe this is for a year or two from now.

Lesley Metz arrives to spend the night. She walks into the apartment just as the sun is streaming into the living room. She stops and says, "I have to cry."

We sit and talk, laughter and tears both flowing freely. She recounts her terror on November 12, as she desperately tried to pull up Joe's record. It all felt surreal, like she was in a movie, with a camera recording her. There was nothing she could do but wait for my call. I remember so vividly the panic in her voice.

Lesley flew out of JFK and lived in New York from 1985 to 1993. We have since determined that she lived in the building that Michael lives in. As daylight fades, we walk along Riverside Park to his apartment. Lesley visits with a former neighbor and the handyman. When we get back home, there is an elderly Asian couple in the lobby, helping each other. "Don't forget the mail, dear," one says to the other. The "dear" tears at me. Why do they get to live out their lives to this ripe old age? Joe and I were going to be model gay senior citizens, the ones about whom people said, "They've been together fifty years." After they get off the elevator Lesley says, "They were so cute." I can only feel anger.

Michael and Sarah arrive for dinner. Michael sets up in the kitchen to cook. I stop to check my e-mail in the back room. There is a long, emotional note from an American Airlines flight attendant. Lesley and I both read it, tissues in hand. She goes out to join Michael and Sarah; I detour into the bedroom and close the door. I pick up the picture of Joe. All of the pain is back. "Why you? Why me? Why? Why? Why?" I make a conscious decision to get off this track. I tell him,

"I'm going to walk out of this room and be with Sarah and Lesley and Michael. I'm going to have a good time tonight in your honor."

And I do—the first dinner party since his death. Michael does a new risotto, Sarah provides the salad. I grill salmon on the terrace. I've managed to take care of some of the "Joe" elements as well. There are olives and hummus for hors d'oeurves; sorbet and cookies for dessert. I light a few candles and put Eva Cassidy, Etta Jones, Clifford Brown, and Gregg Allman on the CD player. I make it through "Over the Rainbow" fairly easily.

On Sunday, I give some of Joe's work things to Lesley: Shoe bags, galley gloves, and a luggage tag that says "AA Crew." She also gets his tape of Princess Di's funeral, and all of his foreign money. As we sort through the money, I realize that I can't recognize English money. This hurts. Joe will never be able to show me London. That was going to be a blast. He, born a loyal subject of her majesty, Queen Elizabeth, showing me, a Mayflower descendent, around my ancestral homeland. I was going to finally taste Indian food and Cobra beer at Kahn's. I would, of course, drag him to the Royal Shakespeare Theater.

Lesley tells me about the time on a London trip when Joe took the microphone before the passengers boarded and sang and danced "Mr. Big Stuff" for the crew. "He was a mesmerizing dancer," she says.

January 14

Lorraine sends an e-mail with the following quote from Carl Jung:

This paradox can be explained if we suppose that at one moment death was being represented from the point of view of the ego, and at the next from that of the psyche. In the first case it appeared as a catastrophe; that is how it so often strikes us, as if wicked and pitiless powers had put an end to a human life. And so it is—death is indeed a fearful piece of brutality; there is no sense pretending otherwise. It is brutal not only as a physical event, but far more so psychically: a human being is torn away from us, and what remains is the icy stillness of death. There no longer exists any hope of a relationship, for all the bridges have been smashed at one blow. Those who deserve a long life are cut off in the prime of their years, and good-for-nothings live to a ripe old age. This is a cruel reality that we have no right to side-step. The actual experience of the cruelty and wantonness of death can so embitter us that we conclude there is no merciful God, no justice, and no kindness. From another point of view, however, death appears as a joyful event. In the light of eternity, it is a wedding, a mysterium conjunctionis. The soul attains, as it were, its missing half, it achieves wholeness. On Greek sarcophagi the joyous element was represented by dancing girls, on Etruscan tombs by banquets. When the pious Cabbalist Rabbi Simon ben Jochai came to die, his friends said that he was celebrating his wedding. To this day it is the custom in many regions to hold a picnic on the graves on All Souls' Day. Such customs express the feeling that death is a really festive occasion. Such is the paradox of my feelings. I haven't decided what death is. This is when I wish I were a good practicing Catholic, and could accept things on blind faith. The torture in our lives is never knowing.

I'm feeling sorry for myself this evening. Having to shop, cook, take care of the cats, clean, all by myself. The cats aren't helping. Ollie is begging for food. Loretta insists on jumping in my lap while I'm eating, even after I repeatedly tell her no.

I'm angry with Joe for leaving me. I'm angry with him for being such a people pleaser, for not facing reality at times in order to keep everything nice. I'm dredging up everything I can to throw at him. Why do I do this? Am I jealous at how much he was loved? Do I wish I had been more like him? Do I feel that I didn't love him enough? Do I think that he would be having an easier time of this if he were in my position?

Arghhh. I don't know. I'm too tired to try and figure it out. I talk with him about all this, but I don't get anywhere. I go to bed.

January 15

I hate having to make the bed myself every morning.

My first book club meeting since November 12. I laugh, I participate, I make jokes. It feels good, except all the while I am conscious of Joe's absence. At one point someone refers to "a bad autumn" and cites 9/11 and Joe's death. I cringe. There is still a part of me that can't believe it and rebels when people use words that confirm it. Earlier in the day, in a routine office meeting, we are talking about a former employee and one of my staff members said, "I saw her at Joe's service." It is so odd to me that for this young person—he is twenty-four—Joe's service is a reference point. What must it be like for survivors of World Trade Center victims to hear the constant drumbeat of 9/11, 9/11, 9/11? Flight 587 has pretty much dropped off the radar screen, but 9/11 has become such a stock phrase in our national dialogue. We hear it all the time and yet, to the survivors, it must be a dagger to the heart, translated each time into "Frank's death," "Susan's death," etc.

Someone says to me after the meeting, "I don't see how you can say that he is gone; he will always be with you." I want to say: Trust me, he is gone. It just ain't the same. I believe in his energy and spirit being present, but it's a far cry from having him physically here. Right now, death is everything. It sucks. I hate it, and I hate the fact that I'm left here alone with this paradox that "Joe will always be with me" and that I am supposed to move on and even "find love again."

Walking home from the 116th Street subway station brings back happy memories. It's all downhill, the final stretch. There's a beautiful view of the steeple of Riverside Church. Home beckons. I don't know if it's better to look up and see a dark apartment, or to see a light on. A dark apartment gives the impression that there is a hole in the building, compared to the lighted apartments above and below. It makes me think of the hole in the north tower of the World Trade Center. But leaving a light on leads to this inevitable brief flicker of hope that he is there waiting for me.

January 16

A sad day. I stay home from work and write. At one point I try, and fail, to take a nap. I have not been able to nap since Joe died. Later I receive a bombshell in the mail: Joe's EZ Pass statement. I am not familiar with these statements, I wasn't aware of the detail they capture. Glancing at it I see a line indicating that he passed through Triborough Bridge toll plaza on November 12 at 5:51:56. This is the last record I have of him being alive.

I completely fall apart. I haven't had one of these no-holds-barred crying jags in a while. When I can speak, I call Sarah and she comes down and sits with me. How can technology capture to the exact second his presence in a tollbooth, and then fail so miserably a few hours later and send 265 people to their deaths? Sarah says, "It's rotten, just rotten."

I don't think Joe was ever late for work. When he had an early sign-in, his ritual would be to count backward from his sign-in time to the time he had to get up. For Flight 587 it would have been: 7 a.m. sign-in, 6:30 parking lot, 5:30 leave the apartment, 4:45 wake-up. In the course of his eighteen-year career with American, I can remember him calling in sick only twice. Shouldn't this count for something? Why didn't his dedication, his precision in assuring that he was always on time, his discipline in reporting to work year after year without absences, protect him? The same questions came up for me when Lesley told me about his singing "Mr. Big Stuff" on the plane. Didn't his gracefulness indicate a way of being in tune with the universe? Didn't it suggest that flight was almost a natural condition for him in a way that it wasn't for others? Shouldn't all this have prevented such a violent, inelegant death?

Apparently not. His death is a fearful piece of brutality, at least as viewed from here. We can't know if Jung's other half of the paradox—the soul attaining its other half and achieving wholeness—has come true.

– IX –

I call Lorraine in the afternoon to tell her about the EZ Pass statement. I'm glad that it's she who answers the phone because I am already blubbering by the time she picks up. This one just plain hurts.

January 21

A strange feeling: The time that Joe has been dead seems longer than the time that we had together. Two months feels longer than twenty-one years. How can this be?

My parents visited over the weekend. As I said good-bye to them today it struck me that I had been mentally preparing myself to help take care of the surviving spouse when one of them died. I had thought about how Joe and I would have to spend more time with the survivor. He would have been generous with his time, perhaps in part to assuage his guilt over not being able to help his own father because of the distance. Now, it is they who are here helping me. As the priest said at Dianne Snyder's funeral: Parents burying children—it's not supposed to be that way.

Dad and I have to work out how to greet each other now. It used to be just handshakes. November 12 changed that. I offer my hand and he goes to hug me. I go to hug him and he offers me his hand.

I bring a picture of Joe into the back room to show him the changes I have made, including the new computer desk. I hold his picture in my lap and tell him about everything. I can't just go ahead and do this by myself. This is our home, he is present in every inch. Every decision we made about it in the past was a joint one.

I hate the fact that Joe is now a folder in my e-mail and My Documents. He is a picture, a statistic, a name on a memorial sculpture, a

86

case number, an estate-to-be in probate (with the lovely name of Estate of Joseph M. Lopes, Deceased). Through me he is a plaintiff in a suit against the State of New York for his worker's compensation benefits. He is a word always on my lips as I try to work him into the conversation. He is a memory that I strive to keep alive. So yes, in this sense he is not gone. But in reality he is. He is gone as my lover. He is gone as my life partner. He is gone as my soul mate, the only person to whom I periodically bared my soul. He is gone as my best friend, the only person to whom I ever attached that label. He is gone as my first reader and muse. He is gone as the first and most enthusiastic taster of my culinary experiments. He is gone as the codesigner and codecorator of our home. He is gone as the coparent to Loretta and Ollie. He is gone as my traveling companion and chief bird scout. He is gone as the far too generous audience for my warbling renditions of "Amazing Grace," "Forever Young," and "The Circle Game."

Friends will fill in for many of these roles. But Joe filled them all. So pardon me while I still hang on to the notion that he is not here with me. Pardon me while I cling stubbornly to the insistence that he is gone.

I threw away Christmas cards today, keeping two from flight attendants. I read both to Joe. A phrase in one card jumped out at me: "Best wishes—you're in my thoughts because I, like so many, know how deeply connected you and Joe were." We were deeply connected. It was a gift, initially, but something we nurtured and fought for to the very end. The writer could have said, "I, like so many, know how deeply in love you and Joe were." This would also have been a true statement, but to me it is not as satisfying as "deeply connected." Lots of things got in the way of those feelings we associate with love. We got angry with each other, we got bored, and we let petty grievances dull our interactions. Our connection, though, was always present. I knew that the anger would ease, the gripes would dissolve, and beneath them would lie the deep bond that we shared. I also knew that if anything threatened that bond we would fight to make sure that it survived. I wondered at times if aging might make us grow distant from each other. But I never feared that the bond would break, only that we would have to work harder to uncover it again. Yes, Joe, we were deeply, mysteriously connected. The note went on to say, "still are—he's definitely still with us, in our hearts." True, but for me the connection is still largely about pain. At some point I hope it can be about something else.

January 22

Things that I still have that were with us from the beginning: His set of pots and pans, a serving spoon from Emporium Capwell, a blanket and quilt from his bed that we slept under on our second night together.

During these cold, dark months, I come home and don't expect much—just dinner, reading, and bed. What I fear is light. How will I make it through a June evening when the eastern wall of the apartment is golden with sunlight and the glow over the Palisades lingers long into the night? I fear warmth—that first spring evening when it's possible to stand looking out over the city in shirtsleeves, when we would have had drinks and dinner on the terrace. I fear beauty, the slow unfolding of the leaves in Morningside Park, the heavy blossoms on the crab apple trees outside the front door, the twinkling of city lights at twilight. How am I going to face all of this without you? How can I live in a world of light and warmth and beauty while knowing that you no longer live in that world?

– X –

A two-hour meeting yesterday with my personal attorney and one from Lambda Legal Defense and Education Fund. I have decided to go ahead with a challenge to the New York State Workers' Compensation Board to get the same benefits I would have gotten had I been legally married to Joe. The survivors of his married colleagues are entitled to four hundred dollars a week for life, or until they remarry. Legally, I am entitled to nothing. His dad will get a $50,000 pay out if my challenge fails.

Some of the ways same-sex partners lose out when a partner dies:

> No option regarding Social Security benefits. All that Joe paid into the system has vanished. If married, I would have been entitled to his Social Security benefit if it were larger than mine.
>
> Joe could not designate me before retirement for a pay out from the company-sponsored pension plan.
>
> I cannot do a direct roll from his 401(k) to mine. I have to take a payout and pay a twenty percent penalty.
>
> With the protection of marriage, property, insurance proceeds, bank accounts, and other items move from the estate of the deceased spouse to the estate of the survivor largely without taxation. Nothing in Joe's estate, of which I am the sole executor, is similarly sheltered.

Joe and I took every possible step to provide for a surviving partner, including signing wills, registering as New York City Domestic Partners, buying our co-op as joint tenants with rights of survivorship, and working for companies and institutions that recognize same-sex

couples. The problems I face are the result of state and federal regula-
tions that limit the definition of spouse to married couples. Defenders
of these laws no doubt believe that they are protecting the institution
of marriage. From my point of view, the argument is illogical. How
does expanding access threaten an institution? The reality is that Joe
and I were married in every sense of the word except the narrow legal
one. We were committed to each other for life. We each became a
part of the other's family. For society to catch up to this reality and
give it legal sanction would not only be fair and just, it would bring
increased visibility and strength to the institution of marriage.

A quiet evening at home. Success in the laundry room. I separate
the clothes into three loads, whites, colors, permanent press. Everything comes out the same color as when it went in. I go to bed without
taking a pill. A few difficult moments when I think about the morning of November 12 and the voice on the radio. Then I stop, roll over,
and go to sleep. I sleep well until 5:30. This is my first good week-
night sleep without medication.

January 24

My first dream in which Joe and I kiss. I wake up, throw the pillow
in the air and yell, "Yeah, we kissed, honey!" Then sadness sets in. I
will only ever kiss him again in my dreams.

When I get home that night, I kiss his picture but, instead of the
usual peck, I press it hard against my lips for a few seconds. Then I sit
down on the floor, roll onto my back, and sob.

Oh, Joseph, how you could kiss. I'm not thinking just of romance.
Kissing was an integral part of your life, in the same way that touching and hugging was. You kissed the cats almost as much as you
kissed me. I loved the way you used to approach me with your lips
puckered, your eyes widening as you closed in as if you were going to
plant a really big one on me. At the last minute you would pull back
and ease in, leaving just the softest impression on my cheek or mouth
(and usually a little nose grease on my glasses). Or the way you
brushed your lips against the back of my neck while I stood at the
sink. I loved the shower kiss, too, big and wet as the water streamed

into my mouth while I said good-bye. And the way at night you would lean over and plant a kiss on my belly before you closed your eyes. Or from a distance, the kiss planted carefully on your index finger and blown at me.

January 26

When Joe was alive, he was not the entirety of my life. I had my writing, my friends, my work, my reading, and my bird watching. Yet his loss feels like it takes up all of my life now.

Last night Michael came to dinner and we were both in sad moods. He said he has noticed this week that I seem down. I think it's true; I am becoming more depressed over Joe's death. It is so relentless. I am tired of kissing photographs. I am tired of only having him in dreams. I feel like a little kid whose blanky has been taken away. Okay! Okay! It's been long enough. Give him back to me now! After Michael left I cleaned up. I told him I wanted to do it alone. I cried through the first part of it. I didn't stop, though, I just took off my glasses so they wouldn't get stained and kept going, filling the dishwasher, putting away the place mats, all the things that we did together after a meal. Eventually the tears just stopped.

It's clear that the Booda Dome isn't working. The seam, where the dome meets the base, is on the outside. This means that when Ollie directs a stream of pee directly at or above the seam some of it leaks out. If the top had been designed to fit into the base, rather than over it, the pee would run into the litter. I'm back to square one. Booda Box and clay litter. When will I ever learn that trying to contain Ollie within some neat and tidy kitty infrastructure is a hopeless proposition?

January 27-28

A drive to Cheshire, Connecticut, to spend the weekend with Wendy, Rick, and the kids. It's a sunny, mild day. Wendy says Jill (age four) talks about Joe, especially when they are driving. "Is he in the clouds?" she asks. Jill asks me if I worked on the same airplane as

Joe. When I try to bring up the subject of Joe with Nate (age seven), he doesn't respond. Wendy thinks he associates it with the World Trade Center and is too hard for him to deal with.

When I get home on Sunday, the car insurance bill is in the mail. It's hard to see the bill in my name. The insurance has been transferred even though the title hasn't been transferred yet. This car, which is so much a reflection of Joe, will soon be in my name only. It's just another in a long line of things where Joe's name gets wiped away. The "we" becomes an "I." I can't stand it; it's like layers of me are being peeled off, slowly, torturously. It's like pulling a Band-Aid slowly off my arm. We learned when we were kids to just give it one quick yank—the pain is worse at first, but it's over more quickly. I can't do that here, I have to remove it hair by agonizing hair.

I have a sad talk with Joe. For the first time I say, "I'm feeling so lonely." I am surrounded by people who love me, but I feel so lonely. I have lost the person to whom I felt comfortable saying pretty much anything. I have lost the person who knew more about me and my family than anyone else. There was such a history there. Everything we said to each other had references to previous conversations, some going back twenty-one years. Joe and I could say to each other, "I'm angry that you said that." "I'm disappointed that you did this." We would eventually find a way to talk it out and reconcile our differences. There was such peace in the reconciliation and sometimes more. At times the outpouring of intimacy and honesty was very erotic.

I can be honest with friends about my feelings, but it's not about something that happened between us. Only with Joe did I have that kind of honesty. It feels like a great loss, right up there with the physical loss. The process of opening up, forgiving, reconciling, moving on, that happens between lovers is gone now. How do I have such a powerful experience in my life again? Or maybe, I don't. Maybe, there is a different kind of experience that I have with friends and family. Or with myself?

By the end of the evening I am calm. Sarah comes over with soup and we watch *Nature* on PBS, a show about the otters of Yellowstone. It's an unusual show in that none of the otters are killed, despite one close call. And no usual warning at the end about how all of this is threatened by human encroachment. We are both relieved that we are let off the hook so easily.

Over the course of the weekend I was aware of several moments when I had not been thinking about Joe, even if only for a few seconds. I'm still not comfortable with this. It still feels like I am abandoning him.

– XI –

Suburban Connecticut, 1962: I'm seven and out canvassing the neighborhood, collecting cans and bottles to raise money for the relief organization, CARE. When we go to redeem the stockpile at the Grand Union, a picture is taken for the *Hartford Courant*. Everyone seems happy except the man at the Grand Union who has to sort the cans and bottles. He starts in on the pile, red-faced and cussing. It's my first exposure to the complex politics of charitable acts.

A few years later, I was back with more complex schemes to raise money for the hungry. I organized backyard fairs, inviting neighborhood kids to come and pay a few pennies to try their hand at a ring toss or crawl through a makeshift fun house. Again, I canvassed the neighborhood to ensure a good turn out. I was not always greeted warmly by my neighbors; sometimes my presence at the door was ignored. Other times I was barely suffered, as if I was a religious proselytizer. My parents looked on with a mixture of bafflement and annoyance as well. Our backyard was taken over for these events. How could my father mow the lawn? After two fairs, I gave up. My friends didn't want to help me and my neighbors stopped coming. This was depressing, as was the realization that the lot of the world's destitute seemed unchanged by the money I had sent so far. Even more dispiriting was the fact that I had had no impact closer to home. Suburban life went on as before.

As I got older, I found other things to do. I tutored kids in reading and taught swimming at a school for the blind. Through church, I got involved in the North End of Hartford, a poor neighborhood that was overwhelmingly black. The civil rights movement had a tremendous impact on me, as did Robert Kennedy's campaign for president. On the morning of June 6, 1968, I awoke to the certainty that Kennedy had won the California primary and now had the Democratic nomination within his grasp. Anne came into my room so that I did not stumble unprepared into the awful news of his assassination. The day of his funeral I sat in front of the television, alone with my grief, watching his funeral train roll past crowds of mourners to his burial place.

Other parts of my childhood were normal—I was a fairly decent left-handed first baseman until opposing pitchers started throwing curve balls at me, and I was voted Class Blusher my senior year—but I was always drawn to what was happening beyond the narrow confines of suburban life. What mattered most was to have something to believe in. I searched for the right cause through college, two years in Washington, DC, and in San Francisco where, to my lasting regret, I found what I was looking for.

It is said that no one ever joins a cult, only delays leaving. In 1980 no one could have convinced me that the quiet, tentative "yes" I uttered to my recruiters would lead to the kind of experience from which I would feel fortunate to escape with my sanity intact, and perhaps even my life. San Franciscans knew the group as the Grassroots Alliance or the Rebel Workers. At times they seemed to be everywhere—circulating petitions, selling their newspaper, handing out leaflets, registering voters. When you spoke with one of them, you couldn't help but notice the intensity and conviction with which they expressed their beliefs. If you worked with them you were struck by the daunting discipline under which they operated.

When I met the group it was spearheading a "Tax the Corporations" campaign, a populist economic proposal to upgrade city services by increasing corporate taxes. It was the "People's" answer to California's infamous Proposition 13. The campaign itself was just the kind of work I had been looking for since my early days of collecting cans. Based in the neighborhoods, it was multiethnic and extraordinarily well organized. It seemed rooted in the traditions of the great American progressive movements—the American Revolution, the labor struggles of the early twentieth century, the New Deal, and the civil rights and anti-Vietnam war movements. The big corporations and their allies in government and the media railed against us. We had the people, though, and we worked furiously to organize them and raise the funds necessary to get our message out. We almost won. On Election Day, 1979, Proposition P received just over forty-nine percent of the vote.

I went to the election night party and stayed until the bitter end. By then only the faithful remained, those who had dedicated their lives to the cause. As people gathered and sang "We Shall Overcome" and other songs, I could feel something very powerful pulsing through the crowd. There was a glow in people's eyes. For a moment I was eight again and Martin Luther King Jr. was speaking from the steps of the Lincoln Memorial. I was a part of something bigger than myself but, this time, I was not sitting alone in my living room in front of a television set. By the end of the evening, I knew that I wanted to join the faithful.

That I wanted to join with this group was only part of the story. The other part was that I had been targeted for recruitment. It was only when I was approached that I learned exactly what it was that I would be joining. It was not the Grassroots Alliance or the Rebel Workers, but the Workers Party. (It would later become the Democratic Workers Party (DWP), a nifty piece of deception since it was anything but democratic, nor did it have many "workers" in it.) The faithful were all members of the Party. The dedication and drive came from the Party. The stellar organizational skills, the salt-of-the-earth slogans and literature, the strategy and vision, all came from the Party. What had looked like a popular rebellion had in reality been largely carried out by a small group of Party cadre, which I was now being asked to join.

The Workers Party was not unknown. It had earned a reputation in its early years as a divisive force that had swept through San Francisco's left and progressive community, sowing destruction in its path. Friends warned me against it. Faced with two contradictory images—one of darkness, of the Party as a narrow, sectarian wrecking crew, and the other of light, of the Party as a broad-minded, dedicated servant to the "People." I chose to believe in the latter image and ignore the former. The Party was clever in its recruitment of me.

The demands on my time and money were modest. Of course, it was hoped I would do more, and I would. I was in many ways the perfect recruit. I was young, looking for direction, and far from home. In March 1980, I signed on to the cause.

By the time I met Joe that October, I was devoting nearly all my time and energy to the Party. We were heavily embroiled in another election campaign with a new version of the Tax the Corporations initiative on the ballot and a full slate of candidates for local office. Improbably, I was one of them. I stood for election to the Community College Board. Joe, meanwhile, was working as the manager of the Tiger Shop at a Macy's in the East Bay. With his brother Tony and his friends Ray and Gary, he was spending a lot of time exploring the bar and disco scene. He was a big fan of the TV show *Dynasty*. While I was off studying and organizing, he and his friends were having *Dynasty* potlucks, at which Joe won accolades for his special Tater Tot casserole.

I spent election night at Joe's house. In the morning we woke to find that not only had I lost, I had finished last among all of the candidates for Community College Board. "That's a first," Joe commented. "I've never slept with someone I voted for."

– XII –

January 28

In the mail at home: Joe's final W2 form and the special issue of *Skyword* dedicated to the crew of Flight 587. I open it right away and turn directly to his page. I'm anxious to get it over with. It is very well done although his birth date is wrong—October 15, 1968. I'm sure he would be pleased that they made him thirteen years younger.

Mostly I am tired of this. I want all of this memorializing to be over. I want all the paperwork to be done. The reality, though, is that with the various lawsuits and challenges, this is going to stretch on for years. Part of me still can't accept this and thinks Joe is going to come back. That's the only way it can really be over, to wipe out all that has happened. The realistic alternative means a processing of forgetting and letting go, something I can't bear to face.

January 29

During my evening talk with Joe I proceed very slowly, with long gaps between words. I suddenly realize that he is not here anymore to finish my sentences. One of the most common things that people said about Joe was that he was a great listener. I heard this a lot from his colleagues. His presence at peer counseling sessions after 9/11 meant a great deal to people. "Joe was such an empathetic listener," the coordinator of those sessions told me. Do I dare say then, that at home, I often found him to be a poor listener? At least initially, anyway. His habit of finishing my sentences was a big issue for me, one that he had to work on for a long time. If he finished one of my sentences, I would say that the answer was wrong, even if it was right. Eventually he learned not to, but it was always a struggle. Sometimes he would raise his hand like an eager student and ask, "Can I finish?" Or, "I know, I know."

This was one of those silly games that couples play, one partner looking for a way to slight the other and gain an advantage. As I became more aware of the dynamic I made sure that I never interrupted Joe, adding to my feeling of self-righteousness. The feeling of not being heard was one that I brought to the relationship and was particularly sensitive about. Joe really was a good listener; sometimes it just took him awhile to tune in. Anyway, it's not an issue now. The picture just stares silently at me. The stage is all mine.

I hear footsteps down the hall and keys outside our door. It is my neighbor going into the apartment next door. This was always the moment at which I could let go of my fears. When the key went in the door, I knew Joe had made it home safe from another trip.

Bumper sticker seen on a car today: 9/11. WE WILL NEVER FORGET. Please, let me forget. At least for a little while.

January 30

Just before going to bed, I detour into Joe's closet. Probably not a good thing to do in terms of getting to sleep, but this time no harm is done. I find a few new things, including his diploma from Columbia, and his CSW (Certified Social Worker) license. I also find a new trove of photographs, including pictures from Lake Winnipesaukee that I don't remember ever seeing. There's a series of three of Joe in the water. He's moving closer in each one until the final one is of him hanging onto the ladder at the end of the dock.

January 31

I make a copy of the Winnipesaukee pictures and send them to Lorraine. An excerpt from the letter I enclose with it:

It always gave me such pleasure to see Joe in the water at the lake. That was true when we first went in 1986, and remained true right through last summer. His presence at the lake meant so much to me because it represented the marriage of my past and present. The lake was so much about family history and my New England ancestry. It was a history I was not always comfortable with, or perhaps I should say, I felt that my ancestry was not comfortable with who I had become. And then I would look out at the water and Joe's head would pop up and I would have this wonderful feeling of happiness. Here was this gay Asian man who was my partner and lover swimming in Lake Winni. And he was loved and accepted by my family. I think I must have feared early on that I would have to choose between who I was and what family tradition dictated I should be. Perhaps that's why I fled to San Francisco in 1978. What was so remarkable was that when we came back East I could see that everyone welcomed and loved Joe. It's a tribute to both Joe and my family. It gives me hope as I confront a new set of fears today.

Why are the pictures of Joe in the water so compelling? Is it because he is buoyant? He can stay up? Like he did (and finally didn't) when flying?

I feel blessed that Joe and I had relatively little unfinished business when he left this earth. We were able to find ways to say most of what we needed to say to each other. One conversation, though, still hangs over me. It started out being about money.

Joe was funny about money. Not so much current money, which we managed smoothly, but future money. He had a need to paint a much gloomier picture about our retirement outlook than was necessary. I suggested once that it was some deeply embedded genetic trait, a leftover from the days when famines racked China. We used to kid about not having enough rice under the mattress. Still, it drove me crazy at times. His 401(k) plan was almost all in fixed-income assets, yet when the stock market dropped he would declare that he had been wiped out. He worried about the size of his 401(k). What mattered was the size of both of our 401(k) plans, I pointed out, to little avail. Although I urged him to, he never created a financial plan. He preferred to live in the land of worry.

One night after dinner, I think it was in October, Joe was standing at the sink loading the dishwasher. I stood behind him. He said in a quiet voice, "Maybe one of the reasons why I feel that I have to have my own nest egg is that I'm afraid that you will leave me for a younger man."

I blew up. "That's never going to happen," I said. "And it makes me angry that you don't trust me more." I walked out of the room. I didn't want to pursue it when I was so angry. I knew that we would get back to it after we had both thought about it for a while. That's what we always did. Besides, I had the rest of my life, and his life, to prove him wrong.

Now I'm left to ponder how seriously he meant it. He did start the sentence with "maybe," didn't he? I'm racking my mind, trying to remember his exact words. It troubles me, but I think my frame of mind now is to focus on anything I can find that is troubling. I have spoken with both Michael and Lorraine about it. I said to Lorraine, "I just hope that when he left this world, he knew how much he was loved." They both assure me that he did, but the fear still gnaws at me. It's little Joey again, wandering alone and afraid, and I didn't do enough to love him and protect him.

In my more rational moments, I know that Joe knew I loved him. We all have fears we never fully overcome; it took great strength for him to tell me this. His telling me was in and of itself an indication of the strength of the bond between us. Still, I'm spending a lot of time these days rewriting that scene in the kitchen. In my mind, I reach over and turn off the water, dry his hands, and lead him to a chair in the living room. I ask him to sit down, while I get down on one knee in front of him.

"Joe Lopes," I say to him, "I love you. I love you now as much, if not more, than I ever have. What we have built together over the past twenty-one years is the most important thing in the world to me. Leaving you for a younger man would be a despicable act. My family and friends would disown me. It would be a legal and financial nightmare. But, all that aside, I don't want to leave you. Not only do I love you, I like you. You are my best friend and I want nothing more than to grow old with you."

– XIII –

I have created folders for all of the paperwork I have: NTSB, life insurance, AD&D Insurance, Joe's documents, Estate, Workers' Compensation, transfers of ownership/cancellations, 401(k), Credit Union. Joe is color-coded and broken out into neat little folders.

Junk mail addressed to Joe from the Animal Medical Center. On the outside of the envelope it says, "It is hard to face the reality of life alone." Tell me about it.

Dinner and theater with Char and Stewart. At dinner I am in a fairly good frame of mind. I am talking about my plans to scatter Joe's ashes. There are at least six places I want to do it. We joke that I might only be able to do a teaspoon at each stop. Stewart tells a story about how he went on an ash-scattering party on a boat and just as the ashes were thrown overboard, a gust of wind came up and blew them back all over everyone. Stewart assures me there will be plenty of ashes. I say, "We don't know how much of Joe we recovered." This is the first time I have said this. It is not the first time I have thought about the condition of Joe's body, but it is the first time I have verbalized the possibility of fragmentation.

Later, at the theater I am laughing hysterically. *Noises Off* is a very funny play. It isn't until the third and final act that I begin to feel sad. Joe would have had to hold onto me to keep himself in his seat at this one. I can feel him gripping my forearm. I find myself not clapping very enthusiastically as the cast members take their bows. Then I have a vision of Joe holding his hands out in front of himself, about chin high, and clapping so enthusiastically. So I do a Joe clap for a while. Later on the subway home I tell Char that I had had a hard time in the third act. "That's not being very fair to yourself," she comments. Everyone wants me to be happy, to let myself enjoy life. I can't just turn it on and off like that.

February 8

Found in his leather jacket this morning: one piece of Trident gum and two little squeeze bottles of lip moisturizer, probably samples. He could never be far from breath freshener, hand cream, or lip care products. I will still be discovering these things years from now.

I spend a few minutes with Chaplain Davis in the morning. "What are my responsibilities to Joe now?" I ask her.

"To cherish the memories you have of him." I tell her about my fears that I still need to care for him. Her answer: "The spirit abides; the soul is at rest." She adds, "I realize that is a paradox."

I talk about how we always struggled to be in synch with each other and now we are out of synch. "He is not here to help me through this," I say. Just as I finish saying it, a large burp erupts from the Poland Spring water cooler in the corner. We both look at it and laugh. "That's never happened before," Jewelnel says.

February 9

Driving to my brother's in Massachusetts, I take advantage of the solitude to scream "NO" once. It doesn't seem to do much good. Screaming is overrated. I listen to some tapes of Joe's I found in his closet. They were probably running tapes. Patsy Cline on one side, Dolly Parton on the other.

I have a good day. At night I go for a walk by myself while my niece Emily is opening her birthday presents. The sadness hits me. For the first time I say out loud, "I am going to die, too, Joe. You just got there before me." I feel this profoundly. Of course, I'm going to die; I know that. But in this context, with Joe having gone before me, it takes on new meaning. When our first cat died I felt that she had been singled out for this fate, that she had been picked on. I feel this, too, with Joe. It's not true, though. His fate is no different from anyone else's; it's just a question of timing.

The stars are brilliant, but also distant and cold. How many billions of people have died and how many have mourned beneath these same indifferent stars? Still, I can't help but ask, "Are you up there, Joe?" as if the soul, once freed from the body, would find a home there.

February 10

I stop on the way home to visit with Joe's colleague, Stephanie Campbell. This is the first time I have been with her other than at a funeral—Dianne's, Barbara's, and Joe's. She lives in an old Dutch Colonial in Fairfield, Connecticut. It is quintessential Connecticut. If Joe had ever visited with her, he would have spent the entire day sitting on the front porch. He loved porches and doors. He would have come back from the visit and said, "We have to have a house like that." Part of him always wanted that suburban experience, a classic house like Stephanie's with a big porch and plenty of room to garden. He wanted to shop in stores with wide aisles and cashiers who actually looked you in the eye and said, "Good morning," and "Thank you."

We walk to the beach. Stephanie has two young daughters and the conversation turns to kids. I am reminded of Joe's favorite cowboy story: A friend of his had a little boy who wanted a cowboy outfit. She didn't want him to have guns, though, so she got him the whole outfit, minus the holster. His dad saw him and asked, "Where's your gun, cowboy?" The little boy answered, "I'm a singing cowboy, Daddy!"

Back at home, a traumatic night. Ollie goes into insulin shock. I pump him full of Karo syrup and give him some canned food with Karo mixed in. He throws up all over the bedroom rug and has two episodes of very wet diarrhea. He has stabilized some when I go to bed. I get up at three to check on him. He is not moving, and I can see that he had more diarrhea. It is smeared all over the floor, and even some on the wall. I pick him up and he starts to wail. He walks around uncertainly, his wails growing increasingly louder and more urgent. I call the vet. The answering service tells me to take him to the Animal Medical Center. I dress, put him in the carrier, and go out and hail a cab on Broadway. The Center is on East 62nd Street, almost to the

FDR Drive. At times during the trip, he is quiet and I fear that he is gone. I put my hand in the carrier and touch him. When we arrive a vet sees him right away. In a few minutes I am told that he is being given oxygen and glucose and is stabilizing. They want to keep him overnight to do more tests.

I refuse to think in terms of, "What would Joe do?" Joe is gone; this is my decision now. We gave Ollie a good life. He was with us for twelve years, the last four as a diabetic. We put thousands of dollars into his care. This is now his third incident of hypoglycemia, the second since Joe died.

I tell the doctor to go ahead with the tests. I'm not ready to let go of him. I get home at sunrise, call in sick to work, and crawl back into bed. I sleep until eleven when the phone wakes me. It's the vet. She says Ollie is doing well.

This had been one of my worse nightmares—an Ollie crisis in the middle of the night when I was alone. What would I do? Now I know. Another human-sized problem confronted.

– XIV –

San Francisco, March 1980, among the faithful—a day in the life of a young recruit to the unDemocratic virtually workerless Workers Party. This was six months before meeting Joe, seven months before the election of Ronald Reagan. The world, as seen from certain select precincts in San Francisco, was still ripe for the triumph of peace, justice, and socialism.

My first official assignment was to the fundraising committee for the new Tax the Corporations campaign. Having lost by only the smallest of margins the previous November, a little extra effort was all that would be required to push it over the top and transform the political and economic situation of San Francisco, and shortly thereafter, the country. I had just settled into a chair at campaign headquarters when the receptionist appeared in the doorway. "Excuse me," she said, fists on her hips. "Did anyone in here just use the last hand towel in the bathroom and not replace the roll?" No one spoke. She stood for a moment, her annoyance growing. "It's extremely disrespectful to everyone who works here to have to go into the bathroom and not have any hand towels. That is not how we run Party facilities. In the future if you use the last hand towel, replace the roll." She turned and left in a huff. I did not volunteer the fact that I had just come from the bathroom. I had not used the last towel because the roll was already empty by the time I got there. Technically I had not broken the rule, but I knew that already, on my first day, I had been bad.

That night I attended the weekly meeting of the fund-raising committee. The room was nearly full when Chris, a campaign manager, entered and took a seat behind the table at the front. Her brow was deeply furrowed and her lips pursed. There were no greetings. Her face contorted into a mask of fury, her eyes narrowed, and she pointed a finger at the man sitting right next to me.

"This is a criticism of you, Ted, for what you did to Ester this weekend. The way you treated her is despicable. She dragged herself into this office on Saturday, dog tired after working all day, to be here to help on fund-raising activities and she sat here for an hour—a goddamn hour—until you got here to give her something to do! She sat here waiting for an hour for you, you son of a bitch!"

Her hand slammed to the table. "You kept Ester, one of our most dedicated and hard-working volunteers, waiting. All because you are too incompetent, too spaced-out to write down when you're supposed to meet someone and show up on time. This is absolutely intolerable. People come to work with this organization because we respect them. They don't expect to come here and sit around the office." Her hand slammed to the table again. "Where do you get off making someone wait for you? Who the hell do you think you are? You think she is going to want to work with an organization that makes her sit around and wait for hours until some young, smart ass college-educated guy decides to show up?"

She stopped and stared, her face scarlet and every tendon in her neck straining. I sat motionless in my chair, my eyes riveted on her. I was unable to glance at Ted beside me. One thought kept repeating itself in my mind like a mantra: These people are very serious. The assault on Ted resumed. Accusations poured bitterly from Chris's mouth. His errors seemed like ordinary human mistakes, but in the context of the criticism they became evidence of sloppiness, arrogance, laziness, flakiness, selfishness, and, most-damningly, petty-bourgeois individualism. Other people began to speak, using this strange new language and building the case against Ted. Finally, after half an hour had passed and everyone had spoken except for me, Chris turned again and faced Ted. Her voice seethed with contempt as she called on him to speak. All eyes turned and I was finally able to look at him. I half expected to see him slumped over in his chair, but he sat upright, his face flushed, but otherwise composed. What he said astonished me.

"I agree with everything everyone has said, and there is even more."

"Yes," Chris interrupted, "let's get it all out."

Ted proceeded to eagerly add to the case against him, outlining occasions that had yet to be mentioned in which he had been late or sloppy in his work methods and had caused extra work for other people. He spoke as if he were a prosecutor presenting a case against someone else. He made no attempt to defend himself or protest anything that had been said. Through it all Chris sat glaring at him. When he was done she resumed speaking. In a quieter voice she told him that he was removed from all responsibilities in the fund-raising unit. He was reassigned to the Party child-care team.

To flee the campaign office and never return would have been the sensible thing to do. I didn't, though. I didn't know that these people who seemed so powerful and righteousness were merely human, and that many of them were tragically flawed. I didn't know then this process of criticism had no redeeming features; it would neither correct my faults nor turn me into an adult. I had to learn the hard way, and it would take almost five years.

The dream was that the DWP would give its members direction and purpose. It would give us the opportunity to participate in something bigger than ourselves. What began as a commitment of one day a week quickly grew until, sometime in the fall of 1981, I surrendered completely. Without acknowledging it to Joe, or even completely to myself, I became a full-time Party cadre. I was fully deployable; when the Party called, I answered. In part, I lacked the courage to say no. I could not refuse an assignment, be it to attend a conference on a Saturday night or work all day Sunday. Everything in the Party was presented with great urgency and seen as a test of character. But it was more than a question of courage. I wanted to be a part of this human machine, a part of making history. At some point I realized I had gone too far down the road to turn back. Either I had to give it up completely—something that was unthinkable—or I had to throw my lot in with the rest of them. I wanted badly to change, to be more sure of myself, to be tougher, to be an adult.

The Party appeared to offer me all that, so I accepted its offer, although with a deep sense of resignation. In accepting I left myself a small escape hatch. I told myself that things would change, that we couldn't keep working at this frantic pace forever. If that did not prove to be true, I would re-evaluate my commitment. The transformation from new recruit to cadre had taken only a year and a half.

The pattern for the next two years of our lives was set. I struggled with the daunting demands of the Party and tried to find as much time as I could for Joe. He bore it as well as any human being could be expected to. At times his anger and resentment broke through, but for the most part he supported me. He believed that it was important to support me in my chosen vocation, but he also believed, he would later tell me, that if I were ever forced to choose between him and the Party, he would lose. As painful as it is for me to admit, he was right. So he chose to bide his time, confident that one day my imprisonment would end. In this he would also prove to be right.

In the spring of 1983, Joe interviewed with American Airlines. In early July he received a call telling him to report to Dallas at the end of the month for training. Although it would later appear to all of us that Joe was destined to fly, the decision to accept the job was a difficult one. He was reluctant to leave San Francisco. When he completed training and prepared to move to Chicago, he wrote to me, "I owe my strength completely to your loving support. Please continue to feed me support and above all, please know that while distance will surely be painful, in my mind, there is no barrier for my feelings for you. In short, nothing will change. I love you more than I could possibly tell you."

I'm sure he meant those words, but we both knew that my involvement in the DWP made the long-term fate of our relationship questionable. In fact, after Joe had been settled in Chicago for a while, he started to date another man, also named Bill. Our relationship may have ended here were it not for a fortuitous bit of timing. Joe later told me that he and Bill spent a Friday night together in Joe's apartment. They were in bed the next morning when the phone rang. I was on the other end. According to Joe, I told him, "I just wanted to call to tell you I love you." The other Bill got the gist of the conversation and was never heard from again. I have no recollection of having made this phone call. The incident remains in my mind one of those mysterious interventions, like the crashing of the window on the day we met.

While Joe was becoming a flight attendant, I underwent my own transformation. In the spring of 1983, I was ordered to quit my job and work for the Party full time. My six-hundred-dollar-a-month stipend came from a variety of scams involving unemployment insurance and disability payments. Later that year, the DWP announced plans for national expansion. In April 1984, I bid farewell to San Francisco and set out on a cross-country caravan to New York.

Over the course of the spring and summer, Joe and I discussed the possibility of his joining me in New York. As he told Lorraine in the letter I now have, it was another gut-wrenching decision for him. In the end, he decided to try it. In August I drove to Chicago, picked him up, and brought him back to New York. Within a few months he found us our own flat in Brooklyn and we once again set up housekeeping together.

It was quickly apparent that we faced the same problem we had faced in San Francisco. The Party demanded all of my time. Only now Joe was separated from his friends and family. He found the New York flying public to be demanding and the commute to the airport stressful. One Saturday in December I came home and found him on the phone to Lorraine. As usual, he was laughing heartily. When he hung up, he came and sat down by me. "When am I ever going to feel settled?" he wondered aloud.

"What do you mean?" I asked, fearing that the conversation I had long dreaded was about to happen.

"Maybe we've reached the end," Joe said. "Maybe we've gone as far as we can go with this relationship."

I marveled at his strength. I knew this could not be easy for him, yet he was calm. He was not going to rush into any decisions. He said that when our lease was up he would think about getting a place of his own.

Again, we were saved. The Party began what would become its final self-destructive spiral. Purges were initiated and in February 1985 I was one of the first to be expelled. When I came home after work one night Joe looked at me and asked, "What are you doing here?" His jaw dropped when I told him that I had stopped working with the

Party. I lied, telling him I could no longer sustain the level of work required.

I was a free man; yet my freedom was a limited one. I had control over my time, but the Party still had a lock on my soul. I expected that I would ask to be reinstated after an appropriate period of time. I was still under the illusion that the Party was a noble calling and that I could be a member and maintain a relationship with Joe as well. In the meantime, we went about our life. We moved to Jackson Heights so Joe could be closer to the airport. I enrolled in a computer programming course.

In November, I received a phone call asking me to come back to San Francisco. The purpose of the visit was left vague. I boarded a plane the next morning. The scene I walked in on was unlike any I had ever seen. The entire cadre had gathered together. But no one ran around shouting orders. No one carried a checklist and gave me an assignment as I walked through the door. Instead, it felt like I had walked into a group therapy session. The previous night, by unanimous vote, the Party had expelled its leader and then disbanded. It will come as no surprise to anyone familiar with groups like these that our leader had been revealed as an alcoholic. That we had been convinced for so long of her brilliance and unparalleled leadership was due to her hold over the small band of middle-level leadership that separated her from the rest of us. They served as her enablers until the very end, when her drinking and abusive behavior reached a point even they could not tolerate. When they finally began to talk truthfully among themselves, an irreversible process was set in motion. Slowly, the circle of truth widened until the entire cadre, including many like myself who had been expelled, were brought in.

Over the course of that November weekend we gathered in informal groups and talked. Emotions swung from jubilation to a palpable fear of the future. What would we do with our lives? How could someone who had answered the cadre call return to normal, everyday living? I felt lucky that I had an eight-month head start on the adjustment process. While some of my former comrades seemed deeply depressed over the sudden change in our lives, my feelings were primarily ones of relief. When not talking, I took long walks through the neighborhoods I had lived in, in a sense reclaiming them. I wandered the Mission and Bernal Heights, and walked a long stretch of 24th Street. Joe was in Phoenix on a layover. I called him and told him that it was over.

I had sworn an oath of secrecy in order to be granted access to the proceedings that weekend, but I quickly abandoned it. Truth telling became a vital part of coming to terms with the Party experience and putting it behind me. Over the next few months I revealed more and more to Joe about the abusive nature of Party life. To this day I feel guilt over the loss of the first years of our relationship and the pain that he had to endure. Once when we were discussing the Party years, Joe told me something that helped ease my mind. It is especially important in light of his death. "As bad as it got, you were always able to let me know that you loved me," he said.

– XV –

Dinner with Michael followed by a *Will & Grace* rerun and the Olympics. Michael asks me if I want to look at the ashes. I've had a Jack Daniels and one glass of wine. I go to the urn and turn it over. The removable panel on the bottom has two screws. I go and get a screwdriver and remove the screws. I slip out the bottom panel and encounter packing material. I remove this and find a plastic bag. It is heavy and bulky and does not easily come out of the urn. Inside the bag is a piece of paper with the name Joseph Lopes and the date of his cremation. Then another plastic bag with the ashes. I can feel them; it is like holding a bag of sand. I decide not to open the bag. I have learned all I need to know. There are plenty of ashes, which to me signifies that most, if not all, of Joe's body was recovered. "You look great, sweetie," I tell him and kiss the bag. We put everything back together and I return the urn to its place. "It's weird, isn't it?" I say to Michael. "That this is all that's left of the body of the man we loved."

February 12

Ollie is home from the hospital with a new diagnosis—hyperthyroidism—and a new kind of medicine. When I let him out of the carrier, he is hyperventilating and unable to walk. His back legs keep giving out on him. I move Joe's ashes and picture over next to where he is lying and ask him to watch over Ollie. I talk for a long time to Joe. I feel his presence with me. I know that it is my mind and my heart that is making the decisions, but he is so much a part of me that it still feels as if we are functioning as a couple. He is right here supporting me.

I detour to his closet. I throw away an airline shaving kit and silverware that he could no longer carry on board after September 11. I keep a can opener and a bottle opener. I arrange a few of his shoes. I'm trying to get comfortable with his closet, working my way up to the day when I begin to dispose of his clothes. I find another Lands' End briefcase with nothing in it. The man of a thousand bags.

February 16

I spend more time rearranging his closet. I remove Joe's clothes from where they hung on the back of the door, fold them up, and put them on the shelf. I put some of my own clothes on the hooks on the door. Now when I walk in I see my clothes and have an excuse to use his closet. It was too sad seeing the same jeans hanging there day after day, unused. They were withering, like the stalk of a plant long since gone to seed.

Michael and I go out to Point Lookout to try to find a black-headed gull. No luck. The planes are close overhead as they land at JFK. This is the closest I have been to JFK since Barbara's service. At one point an American Airlines 767 glides by. Perhaps from London. How many times did Joe come home safely on exactly that flight, perhaps even that plane? I used to feel such happiness and pride seeing an American plane on this approach. Now it fills me with sadness.

February 17

Curtis comes over to help me crank out letters. Cancellation of Joe's Banana Republic and Sears credit cards. Letters to Verizon, Sprint, Time Warner, EZ Pass, and Citibank safe deposit box asking that all accounts be transferred to my name. ME! ME! ME! The *we* shrinks a little further.

I have to sign these letters "William S. Valentine as Executor of the Estate of Joseph Lopes, Deceased." I can't stand to look at it. I hate the presence of the word deceased. It seems so unnatural following Joe's name. There are some names it would look quite good after.

"Why can't we be writing Slobodan Milosevic, Deceased?" I ask Curtis.

February 18

President's Day. The end of a three-day weekend. I miss you something fierce today, my darling. It's dusk, the candles are lit, and the lights of the East Side are beginning to twinkle in the distance. I'm sitting in the living room. It's been a pretty good weekend, but today I began to weaken. It started in the laundry room. Another round of yellow underwear. Fifteen pairs of briefs, all brand new, washed for the first time. I tried to bleach them, but it didn't really help. This is when I started feeling sorry for myself in a major way. If you were here none of this would be happening. It didn't help that while I was waiting for my newly yellow briefs to finish drying I read a notice on the bulletin board that one of our fellow Morningside Gardens residents had passed on at the age of 106. She lived in three centuries. She was granted twice the years you were, and then another sixteen.

When I really started missing you, though, was when I went shopping for dinner. I went to get a bottle of wine and the thought hit me that I would never again buy you a bottle of wine and watch you taste it. No more swirling it around in the glass, taking a big sniff, and then swishing it around in your mouth. I can just hear you say, "Oh, that's nice. Very nice." You would say that even if it wasn't, just because I bought it for you. Remember the first time we ever ordered a bottle of wine in a restaurant? It was 1985 at Lake Tahoe. We ordered a bottle of Sutter Home White Zinfandel. I think we paid twenty dollars for what was probably a four-dollar bottle of wine. We thought it was the height of sophistication.

February 19

A small crisis at work. For most of the morning I am focused on this; Joe recedes a bit into the background. Still, his death is like the air on a humid day—I can't help but be aware of it, even if I am not thinking directly about him.

Going forward without him: Chaplain Davis says that I can't. He is part of me. Maybe going forward with him means living my life. He is a part of me, so much of me has been influenced by him. More than eighty percent of my adult life was spent in a relationship with Joe. This is how I honor and respect him—by living my life, wherever it takes me.

Late in the day I receive a call from Michael. I pick it up and spontaneously answer in the way I often would when Joe's calls came through. It's a variation on "hello" that he picked up somewhere along the way. It sounds like "Yeah-low," with the "low" strung out and the voice rising at the end. We would go back and forth three or four times before getting down to the business of the call. I had forgotten all about this. It just dropped out of my life on November 12, as did seeing our home phone number coming across on the caller ID screen on my work telephone. How many other endearments, habits, and ways of interacting disappeared that day?

E-mail from Lorraine: I tell [Joe] all the time that we will always look after you for him.

I receive a check for $10,000 from the Wings Foundation, a foundation created by American Airlines Flight Attendants.

Steve comes over for the day to watch Ollie and try to get a urine sample so we can check his blood sugar. I suggest that he bring the cast recording to the play *Urinetown*. He tries singing instead. Only when he sings "Moon River" does Ollie jump in the box to pee.

February 20

A picture of President Bush in China with Chinese Premier Jiang Zemin. Joe used to point to pictures of Jiang and say, "Look at his hair. See that shoe-polish black? That's what I'm going to look like when I have my hair colored."

February 22

You would have been so proud of your little boy last night, Joe. Ollie had to go to the vet for a follow-up on his hyperthyroidism. He was on the table for a long time, including a shaving and three at-tempts to draw blood. (The last one was successful.) He didn't protest a bit. He was a complete trooper. Dr. Fierman declared him Cat of the Month on the spot.

– XVI –

February 23

Lorraine calls this morning to say that Joe has finally appeared to her in a dream. He was trying to make her laugh, which he was so successful at in life. I am happy for her. She had felt bad that both her daughter, Zoe, and I had had dreams in which he appeared, but she hadn't. Let's hope it's just the beginning.

I always feel the urge to try to make her laugh in the way that Joe did, but I can't do that. She had more than forty years with him. They had a whole rich history together stocked with memorable characters, nicknames, accents, and pet phrases. Joe called on all of this to keep her laughing.

It's Saturday morning, and as I poke around the apartment I am aware of all the house rules I can break now. I don't have to immediately replace the bag in the trash can after taking the trash out. Even better, I don't need to shake out the bag so that it opens fully. Joe took great umbrage at putting something in the trash only to find that it sat at the top because I hadn't fully opened the bag. I can leave the hand towel wherever I want instead of returning it to the handle on the stove door. I used to get in trouble for all of these things. I'm also aware of how quiet the apartment is. On weekends, if his allergies were acting up, Joe would often emerge from the bedroom Felix Unger–like—dripping, snorting, and sneezing.

February 25

Something has changed. I am more focused on myself and not so much on taking care of or protecting Joe. In the past I felt I had to stay with the pain to be with Joe. Now I stay with the pain because it is my way of going through the process. And the reality is that the pain is not as intense. Initially, I tried to keep the apartment exactly as we had it, even carrying out plans we had made, but hadn't gotten to yet, like painting the hall. Now I am thinking about making changes that I know I wouldn't be able to do if Joe were still here.

There is an irony in my having painted the hallway the color that Joe picked out just before he died. Earlier in our relationship, around the time we were in couple's counseling, I used to fantasize about having my own place. I didn't want to break up with Joe; I just wanted to have my own space. In a sense, I wanted to achieve physically what we had to do emotionally—separate ourselves from each other and define boundaries. The triumph of our therapy was to be able to do that while still living under the same roof. In my mind's eye, I had a picture of the hallway of my own apartment. Just of the door and the wall, the area that I would walk into when I came home. The color of that wall was very similar to the color Joe picked out.

February 28

I pay off the mortgage via wire transfer this morning. Last week the car was paid off. Using the $150,000 in life insurance Joe left me, I am debt free. I am relieved, but can find little to celebrate in this. This was planned to happen in 2005 or 2006. I'm sure we would have had a big celebration then. Thank you, Joe, for leaving me enough money to take care of this.

I feel oddly adrift, unmoored from the anchor that was Joe's love. I can come and go as I please, and no one knows. Walking to a meeting I see two old men on the streets. One has a walker and is just standing by a building as if he can't go on. The other is leaning over a trash can, vomiting. Strings of saliva and vomit hang from his mouth and twist in the wind. I am terrified of ending up like this.

March 2

In the morning I answer a call for "Joseph Lopes." I ask who is calling. Sears Appliance Center, I'm told. Our refrigerator is from Sears. "Mr. Lopes is deceased," I say. I hate the words as I say them.

Mr. Lopes makes him sound like an old man. *Deceased?* Why not just say *dead.* Even *passed away* is better than deceased. "Is there a Mrs. Lopes?" she asks. "I'm Mrs. Lopes," I answer. I don't want to go into it. "There is no Mrs. Lopes," I say and hang up.

I plunge into the heart of music sentimentality by listening to a tape of Joe's that predates our relationship. The liner is faded and yellow. In his handwriting, printed and capitalized: SIDE A: JEAN-PIERRE RAMPAL/ CLAUDE BOLLING, "SUITE FOR FLUTE AND JAZZ PIANO." SIDE B: PACHELBEL KANON—ALBINONI ADAGIO. This was Russian River Music. Driving down River Road from Hwy 101 toward Guerneville, about an hour and a half north of San Francisco, we loved to listen to this tape. Pachelbel was the main attraction. For years afterward, when we found a nice country road we would refer to it as Pachelbel territory. Eventually, like many, we ran the Kanon into the ground. But it held such strong sentimental attachment for us that I don't think either one of us really ever tired of it, except perhaps at weddings. We never had a wedding, but in some ways it was our wedding music as well. As much as any piece of music it reminded us of our beginnings and what was for both of us a beautiful gift. I am okay listening to it. Actually, it makes me happy.

A busy weekend. Friday night, Stewart, Curtis, Juan, Sarah, Bob, and John come for pizza and a viewing of the video of Joe's service. On Saturday, two old friends, Linda and Lynn come with dinner. On Sunday Michael invites me down for dinner. I decide to drive. I'm worried about the car not getting any exercise. My new book, *Car Smarts,* has arrived and the first thing that jumped out at me as I skimmed through it was a tip to run the air conditioning periodically. I'm nervous about driving, particularly about trying to find a parking spot. As I walk to the car, I'm thinking about the day of Joe's service and how Rosemary saw her seven-hundredth life bird while she was praying for me. Just as I am thinking this, I hear a fluttering of wings in front of me. I recognize the white-edged tail feathers of mourning doves. Three of them settle in a tree nearby. "Oh, Joey, is that you?" I ask, looking skyward. Perhaps he is telling me I'll have no trouble driving and parking. That's the way it works out. There's a big fat space waiting for me right by Michael's apartment building. I make it in on the first try.

March 5

Joe's last paycheck arrives. I had been anticipating it, but I wasn't quite prepared for the word "final" everywhere. I am required to sign an affidavit stating that I am the executor of Joe's estate and agree that these will be the final wages he receives from his employment at American Airlines. Two paychecks a month for eighteen years—more than 430 paychecks. I throw it on the table and yell out, "I don't want his fucking final paycheck! I want him!"

March 6

I am ready to take on the Department of Motor Vehicles. I have read through all of the materials on the Web site, downloaded the forms, and filled them out and called ahead to make sure I have everything I need. I arrive at the Harlem branch fifteen minutes before opening. Forty-five people are already in line in front of me. I appeal to Joe for strength. This was his realm; everything I do with the car is new for me. I look up in the sky and notice a hawk circling overhead a few blocks north. I can't really tell, but it's probably a red-tail. Thank you, Joe. I will be strong.

The doors open at 8:30 and I am immediately routed to a counter. I turn over my documents—letters testamentary, death certificate, title, insurance card, two forms, and a document from the bank indicating that I have paid off the loan. A few minutes later I write out a check for $80.50. I am handed a new set of license plates, a registration sticker, and a temporary inspection sticker. I'm out of the office by 9:00. I stop at Krispy Kreme and pick up two donuts. At home, I put Joe's picture up on the table as I have my donuts. "The car is in my name, sweetie," I tell him. "But in my heart it will always be your car."

– XVII –

"I would like to lead a more normal life now," I wrote in 1986 to a friend who had watched with concern as I was drawn into the Party. That normalcy would have to wait, though. I had reasons for staying in the DWP long after I wanted to, to subject myself to its abuses, and to put my relationship with Joe at risk. I couldn't write it all off to youthful idealism. As painful as Party life was, it was also a shelter from personal demons. Now I had lost that shelter. Finally freed from the DWP and able to exert some control over my life, I promptly fell apart. Finally able to devote time to Joe and develop our relationship, I attempted to have an affair with a man seven years younger than I.

I made eye contact with him on the E train on the way home to Jackson Heights. He followed me off at my stop and we went to a bar. By the end of the evening, I was deeply infatuated. All I wanted from him was passion; I had little interest in a long-term relationship. He had different ideas, though. He had been burned once, and was unwilling to get involved with anyone again without being certain that the other person was available. I plunged in anyway, probing for weaknesses in his defenses. I lied to him about my relationship with Joe, hinting that it might be over. Was what I wanted so unreasonable? Wasn't that what gay men did? Apparently times had changed; he held the line.

I told Joe early on about the affair. I didn't want to deceive him. In typical Joe fashion he was overaccommodating. Rather than throw me out of our bed, he offered to sleep on the couch. Once again, he would bide his time and wait patiently for me to come to my senses. "Did you want him to fight harder for you?" Al asked me later. At the time I didn't know what I wanted. Affairs are stupid, hurtful ways of pointing out problems with relationships and that, in the end, is what this one accomplished. After about six weeks, my infatuation began to fade. I went away to my family's cottage for a weekend. While I was there I called Joe and apologized and told him the affair was over. Instead of having the fling I felt I so desperately needed, I entered therapy.

I thought therapy would last a few weeks, a few months at most. I wanted to understand the affair I had just attempted, as well as my Party experience. I ended up spending eight years in therapy, including a year and a half with Joe in couple's therapy. Along with loving Joe, I consider therapy to be the most profound and hopeful experience of my life. That's the view from this side, though. While I was undergoing it, therapy was often enormously painful. There was one overriding issue that I would struggle with again and again, one that deeply affected my relationship with Joe—my experience as a survivor of childhood sexual abuse.

On a warm summer day in the late 1950s I followed a neighbor into his house. I was four or five years old, and when someone older asked me to do something, I did it. We entered through the garage and went into the basement. Larry closed a few doors and I waited in the middle of the room. I was not sure of his age, other than that he was a teenager and much bigger than I.

What happened in that room started innocently enough. Larry was interested in my body. I was curious about his. I felt special, I wasn't used to having this much attention directed at me. I have clear and specific memories of the sex games he initiated me into. Then the sense of initial excitement began to change to confusion as the games got stranger. I didn't know what was happening; I was a little frightened. Larry was still gentle and playful, still a kid like me, but he was leading me into areas that I knew nothing about.

It is here that my memories of that day were interrupted. When my memory resumed I was fully dressed. Larry was too. He gave me two Hershey bars and stroked the back of my neck. I looked at the floor.

"You won't tell anyone?" he asked. I shook my head no. I was sent on my way home. The final memory is in the backyard, walking home alone. I knew that I would never tell anyone, because I was sure to bear at least part of the blame. And how would I even describe what Larry and I did? No. What had happened between us was our secret.

When I began therapy I told Al about my sexual abuse history. I gave him a bare-bones description of the incident. At that point I believed that it was the therapist's job to judge what was important or not, and to tell me what to do. Al said little, and we went on to other things. Several years passed before the issue came up again. One night I was watching television and saw two young women being interviewed on a talk show. They were describing their experience of having been molested as children by their father. There was nothing in particular about the women's stories that I connected with, but I continued to listen. Suddenly I found myself crying. The source of my emotions was clear to me: in my mind I had a vague image of myself in the basement. For the first time since that day a palpable feeling connected to the incident existed.

At my next therapy session I said to Al, "I've had some feelings come up regarding my sexual abuse experience." I was going away on vacation and wouldn't see him for a few weeks. I only wanted to signal that this had happened and that I would turn my attention to it I when I came back. My question that night was simple: Was this something he could help me with? As was often the case in therapy, it seemed a silly question. One part of me knew that therapists deal with sexual abuse issues, but another part of me didn't know, and needed to ask. Therapy worked when I paid attention to the latter, not the former, voice, so I tried to ask, "Can you help me with this?" I could barely get the words out; my body shook with sobs. When I could talk, Al asked me what I was feeling. I spoke of needing to know if he knew about sexual abuse, if he had worked with other clients regarding this issue. He quickly said yes, as I knew he would. What was important, though, was not that I received the answer I expected but that he acknowledged the importance of the question. This was a moment when the abused child's presence in the room was palpable. His expectations were that Al would look at me with a kind of blank look in his face, as if to say, "What are you talking about?"

Without even having begun to discuss the details of the abuse, a window had opened onto the feelings I had experienced. If what I felt in the room with Al was a reflection of what I felt when I was molested, then telling anyone about it was out of the question. I did not understand what was done to me, and did not believe that anyone else could understand it either. I felt utterly alone in what I had endured; I was a citizen of a private world. If I tried to communicate my experience to others, would they even understand the words as I spoke them? There was a second fear reenforcing this first one. Even if someone did know what I was talking about, wouldn't I be blamed for this anyway? Wasn't I to some degree complicit? Since I didn't stop it, why complain about what happened?

One of the remarkable things about therapy was its capacity to tap into frozen emotions. During one session with Al, I revisited the feelings I had experienced as I was being sent home from my neighbor's basement. He paid me with candy bars, extracted my pledge of silence, and sent me on my way. I struggled for the words to convey to Al the depth of the humiliation I had felt. Finally I blurted out, "He took away my dignity." When I said the word *dignity,* I fell apart. During those final moments, when my neighbor was purchasing my silence, it seemed to me that he had looked inside me and concluded that I did not have it within me to tell on him. At the time, I could only conclude that he was right. I experienced this as a failure on my part. Thirty years later, I could see it differently. It was a question of power, an act of aggression committed against a weaker party. First he violated the physical boundaries of my body, then he violated the emotional boundaries of my soul—"You won't tell, will you?"

As I spoke with Al I felt the usual mix of feelings—pain and an overwhelming sense of sadness for the child who had to go through such an experience alone. I expected the crying jag to run its usual course, but this one took a different turn. Suddenly my right arm was alive, almost twitching. The fingers on my right hand splayed out, as if I was reaching to grasp something. Or perhaps to strike someone. A different emotion was present now. It did not wash over me as much as burn within. It was anger, even rage. I marveled at its presence—I was angry! I was equally surprised at the object of my anger. It was clearly directed at my neighbor for what he had done to me.

To feel anger at my neighbor was monumental because for as long as I could remember, my feelings toward him were ones of adulation. In order to survive my sexual assault incident, I had "forgotten" the traumatic parts. I remembered only that he had paid attention to me. He had made me feel special. In truth, I was sexually attracted to him. That I should love the boy who abused me, rather than hate him, was a source of considerable shame and confusion for me. Yet the image of my neighbor as a golden boy, a long-sought lover, was one I had carried for decades. My development into an adult did not alter it. It was not until I said the word *dignity* that the image of my neighbor began to crack. Now a different picture of him emerged—abusive, manipulative, conniving.

My hope was always that with a few cathartic sessions like this one the suppressed memories of my abuse experience would come flooding back and I would be able to put the issue behind me. Therapy offered no quick fixes, though, and before I could get "better" I had to get a lot worse. Within a year of seeing Al, I had started experiencing severe panic attacks and a lower-level, day-to-day anxiety. The anxiety went on for five years. The panic attacks were infrequent but terrifying visitors. They were frightening for Joe, too, who was present for several of them. I also found that issues surrounding my sexual identity came to the forefront. The streets were full of teenage boys who reminded me of my neighbor. At times I felt a desperate attraction to these boys. I had no desire to be in a relationship with any of them, but it was difficult for me to abstain from casual sexual relationships with young men, and, on two occasions with teenage boys. It was easy to have quick, anonymous encounters in the gyms and parks of Manhattan, or on the piers of the West Village. Joe deserved and wanted a monogamous relationship. I wanted to give him one, but when I couldn't, I didn't hide it from him. He knew that I was struggling with this issue and it was his decision to give me some room to work it out. We kept talking, and in our conversations we came to an agreement about how to remain faithful to each other.

Al and I kept talking, too. We spent a lot of time exploring the memories that I had of my abuse experience and one of the most interesting things we discovered was a distinct difference existed between the images of the first part of the abuse and those of the second part. The images at the end—when I was getting paid with candy bars and sent on my way home—all came from above, as if shot from a camera on the ceiling. I came to call this part of me that split off and watched from above the *ceiling child.* Initially, I judged him harshly—he had colluded in his own abuse; he did not have the courage to tell; he was a hollow shell, all brain, no body.

Al had a different view, which he shared with me during one session. "That's not how I see him at all," he said. "In that child is the essence of the child—the soul. He took what was essential away from the body to protect it."

Al's use of the word *soul* began to change my understanding of the ceiling child. He was not hollow, but soulful. All week long I had images involving the child on the ceiling. In one image an adult was reaching to the ceiling and taking the child down. There was something odd, though, in the image. The child was translucent. This troubled me, and told me that I wasn't quite ready for a true rapprochement with him. That would have to wait several weeks.

That year I watched the Peter, Paul, and Mary Christmas concert on public TV. Toward the end of the concert a group of children came on stage and a candle was lit. A man passed the light to a young boy, and as he did the camera captured the look on his face and the boy's. The man's face was full of compassion, the boy's, joy and expectation. At that moment a tremor went through me. I passed into one of the long, cathartic crying sessions that usually took place in therapy. At my next session as I told Al about what had happened I was transported back to the same feelings I had experienced while watching TV. Only this time I knew I was crying for myself, for the child on the ceiling. I struggled to get out a sentence in my head. It was a tribute to the ceiling child, a metaphor that allowed me to see him differently and embrace him. Finally, I got the words out. "He kept a candle burning."

At this point the session was transformed into one unlike any I had ever had. Neither Al nor I said more than a few sentences. I felt no compulsion to fill in the gaps and had none of the usual fears about saying the "right" thing. I had to keep shifting in my seat and flexing my hands to keep from going numb. A lot going was on with my body, and that seemed appropriate. The issue at hand was the reunification of the ceiling child with his body. I had no awareness of time passing and was startled when I looked at my watch and saw that the session was over.

What was the significance of the particular words, "He kept a candle burning"? The candle's flame is fragile and vulnerable, and yet it burns on. In doing so, it symbolizes resistance. I had always viewed the ceiling child as weak, as having colluded in his own abuse. Now I could see that the very creation of the ceiling child was an act of resistance. It was, as Al had said, a way of taking my soul, or essence, to a place that was protected from the abuse my body was experiencing. My neighbor thought he had purchased my silence when he asked, "You won't tell, will you?" He interpreted the nodding of my head as acquiescence, but that was only my body speaking. He did not know that above him on the ceiling a different answer was given.

The ceiling child was fragile, and given other factors his memory could have been extinguished. But he survived until I could return as an adult and find him. Then I could say in response to my neighbor's question, "Yes, I will tell."

In my first session with Al I had asked, "How will I know when it's over?" I needed to see my way out before I would commit to this process. His answer of, "We'll both know," was hardly reassuring. It proved to be accurate, though. The day finally came, in May 1994, when I walked into Al's office, sat down, and said, "I'm ready." He smiled. It had been eight long, arduous years. Even Al, who had always maintained that time was irrelevant in therapy, admitted that it had gone on longer than he thought it would. His assertion that therapy could never undo the hurtful legacies of the past but that it could change my relationship to them also proved to be true. At my worst moments I feared that the sexual identity forged in my neighbor's basement would remain frozen and that I would spend my adult life pursuing current-day incarnations of him. I was able to leave therapy because I knew this was not true. One of the things that made me most happy as Al and I wrapped up was to speak about my feelings toward Joe. In our fourteen years together he had endured the Party experience, years of daily battles with anxiety and panic, and my turbulent search for a sexual identity. At times in our relationship I felt that we stayed together because we were both afraid to make a change. That was no longer the case. Our connection was real. Although the issues surrounding my sexual identity would live on, they were no longer a threat to my relationship with Joe. "This is for life," I told Al. It was a great relief to me that I could finally say this, and do so with pride, happiness, and as much certainty as any human being was capable of.

At the final session, Al shared with me his feelings about our ending. "I want you to know what it has been like for me to sit here through this with you," he said. "You opened yourself up; you made yourself vulnerable. I will feel your loss greatly. But I want you to know that I will deal with it, that I will feel the sadness, but I will survive it and go on. And I'm really glad that I can tell you this."

He was clearly emotional, in a way that I had never seen before.

"Although this is ending, in a way it will never end," Al said. "I will live on in you and you will live on in me. In fact, you will live on in me in one very specific way." He told me that for several years he had been leading groups for health care professionals who work with AIDS patients. As part of the training he had used a story I had written that dealt with loss due to AIDS.

"It is always one of the most powerful parts of the group, for them as well as for me."

I was surprised and touched by this. To the very end, therapy took unexpected turns.

I believe that if I had not been sexually abused as a child, I never would have met Joe. I can't prove it, of course, but I now see the journey that took me to San Francisco as a direct result of my sexual abuse experience. I was searching for a way to live on as little money as possible. Therapy helped me see that this life project, evident as early as age seven when I started collecting cans and bottles for CARE, was a legacy of the confusion I had felt at having received my first paycheck—two Hershey bars—for performing sexual favors at age four. Money was tainted from that point on and San Francisco appealed to me as a place where I could live communally and far from the galloping consumerism of American society. Once in San Francisco, the other legacy of my abuse experience kicked in. I had to find someone with a body type similar to my neighbor's, or at least to the image I had created of his body. Because of his Asian heritage, Joe's body, even though he was twenty-four, fit the bill.

In a very real sense, then, my sexual abuse experience brought me to Joe, and attracted me to him. Good came from bad. Then, the legacy of my abuse experience threatened to destroy our relationship. This pushed me into therapy, which led to couple's counseling and a great strengthening of our relationship. I was forty when therapy ended and I hoped we had reached something of a plateau and could reap the benefits of years of struggle. The tragedy of Joe's death derailed that hope and brought me back to therapy, where I found that all that I had been through before in confronting my sexual abuse history now prepared me for what I had to face.

I spoke with Al by phone late on the night of November 12. He had not seen Joe in more than a decade. "I've worked with hundreds of men in therapy," he said, "and Joe was one of the gentlest I ever met." I went to his office two days later and poured out my darkest fears to him. I gave him a copy of "Widow's Watch" and told him that I was afraid that I had brought down Flight 587. I told him about the fantasies I had had in which I eulogized Joe. I also spoke of feeling special and of having been chosen for this pain. The latter issue was a familiar one from the work we did regarding my sexual abuse history. Al listened intently, as he always had. "Your fears are not that powerful," he told me. Regarding my eulogy fantasies he said, "We all do that. I hate to bring things down to the banal, but we do." Al told me that when Joe and I were in couple's therapy he had spent a long time looking for feelings of conflict regarding our relationship on Joe's part. After a year he concluded that there were none. "That doesn't mean that there weren't issues, there were. But his feelings of love for you were unambiguous. He was a real prize. And that's going to make this process all the more difficult."

At the end of the session Al wouldn't let me pay him. He asked to attend Joe's service and as I stood to leave, he hugged me. This was all very different from the therapy of old. In some ways it wasn't even therapy. After seeing Al for six sessions, I decided to stop. It was clear to me that this was not what I needed to do now. There were no secrets that I could reveal only to him. Even my darkest fear—that I was somehow responsible for Joe's death—was something that I had spoken about with others. I was doing what I needed to do—grieving, crying, writing, and trying to go on living. This was my full-time job right now. Al quickly agreed that therapy was not necessary.

It was important for me to see Al after Joe's death. It was important for me to reconnect with the man who helped me through so much pain. More than needing therapy I needed to reconfirm what I learned the first time: That I would always feel this pain, but that it would eventually be different. That the only way to transform the pain was to go through it. That I did not need to fear fear, but could sit with it and survive it.

In our last session Al drew an analogy between my sexual abuse experience and Joe's death, saying both will always be with me. He then laughed and said, "That's a terrible analogy. Forgive me."

I understood what he meant. The abuse was terrible and I wish it had never happened. It certainly hindered my relationship with Joe. It is still with me, but it is different. I shared with Al another way in which the analogy was interesting. It was during the exploration of the ceiling child that I developed a sense of having a soul separate from my body. That experience gave me hope for the continued existence of Joe's soul and the possibility of my experiencing it.

There was one nugget I took away from my last session. Al told me, "Sometimes we try to give to others what we can't give to ourselves." We were talking about my feelings that I failed to protect Joe in life and that I still needed to protect him in death. Al suggested that the trauma of Joe's death had brought back many of the issues that had surfaced in therapy. One of the most persistent was protecting Joe. There was a part of me that always wanted to see Joe as little Joey and to take care of him. It was easier than taking care of the ceiling child. "Joe was always perfectly capable of taking care of himself," Al said. This was true, a reality that his getting on a doomed plane doesn't change. No amount of protection could eliminate all risk from his life or mine.

After the session I caught the E train uptown. At 42nd Street I got out to wait for the A train. While I was waiting a C pulled up on the local track. At the last minute I decided to jump on since there were seats available. I sat down and looked up. Above me was a poster from the Poetry in Motion series. It contained an excerpt from one of my favorite poems, Wordsworth's "Ode: Intimations of Immortality from Recollections of Early Childhood":

> What though the radiance which once was so bright
> Be now ever taken from my sight,
> Though nothing can bring back the hour
> Of splendour in the grass, of glory in the flower;
> We will grieve not, rather find
> Strength in what lies behind;
> In the primal sympathy
> Which having been must ever be;
> In the soothing thoughts that spring
> Out of human suffering;
> In the faith that looks through death,
> In years that bring the philosophic mind.

– XVIII –

March 9

Thirty-one thousand feet aboard American Airlines Flight 721 to Dallas. It is very choppy, but I am calm. I did not expect to be afraid, and I am not. There is little to fear now. If I die, then whatever fate awaited Joe awaits me. I'm excited about taking this trip. Lately I have been feeling that the weight of sadness has lifted somewhat. I am less aware of Joe's absence and more aware of his presence. He lives on through me, and by going on with my life I keep him alive.

A conference in Las Vegas has given me the excuse to travel, and I have added stops in Dallas and Tucson to my itinerary. Some of Joe's ashes are in a container in my luggage. The Ashes Tour has begun.

Lesley Metz picks me up at DFW. Her house is tucked into a little parcel of land on a quiet street. It's a small brick bungalow. When we visited in May 2001, Joe spent a lot of time on the front porch, dreaming, no doubt, of the day when he could sit on a porch just like this and call it his own. Inside, the kitchen walls are covered with salad servers and bowls, all made by Lesley. Now she's involved in illustrating a children's book. Two more clues about why Lesley and Joe hit it off so well: As we're sitting down to lunch, she asks, "What should we do for dinner?" Then later, after we had dinner, which included asparagus, she emerges from the bathroom and calls out, "asparagus pee." I had already visited the bathroom, and felt a twinge of sadness as I realized that this was another thing I had lost from my life. With Joe's fondness for word play, asparagus became "a spare goose." "Whew! There's a spare goose around here!"

I am meeting Josie the cat for the first time. The week of Joe's death, she appeared on the front porch of the house of Lesley's friends,

Kylie and Anthony, a few doors down. Their house is also a bungalow. When Joe and I took a walk around the neighborhood in May, he had seen their house and said, "That's it. That's the one I want." Josie took up residence on the wicker chairs, just where Joe would have. Initially she was named Joe, then Josie, when her plumbing was checked. After a few weeks with Kylie and Anthony she moved down the block and adopted Lesley.

On Sunday Lesley buys a bench to put in the backyard in Joe's honor. We set up the bench and open up two cold beers. I get the ashes ready. Josie is watching longingly from the kitchen door and Lesley relents. "Just for a little while," she says as she opens the door. A few weeks ago her cat Casey disappeared and she is determined to keep Josie an indoor cat. Lesley points out a spot where a previous cat is buried. I stand over it with the ashes.

"Well, dear boy, I've brought you here because I know how much you loved Lesley and this house and I think you would like to be here with her kitty. Dallas is where you began your flying career. And even though flying took you from us, we know that it was what you loved and what you were meant to do." I empty out the urn. We return to the bench to finish off our beers.

Josie has been staying close, exploring the backyard. She meanders over behind the toolshed. After a few minutes, Lesley calls for her. When she does not appear, she gets up and goes to look behind the shed. "She's gone," she says when she emerges. There's a gap beneath the fence that leads out to the alleyway. We walk up and down the alleyway, looking for her. Lesley returns to the house to get some treats, I ask for a flashlight to check under the shed. Another ten minutes passes without Josie. Lesley's worried now. "Not again," she says. "I couldn't stand it if I lost her, too."

I pull Joe's bench over to the fence between Lesley's house and her neighbors' and stand on it. There's Josie looking back up at the fence. Looking across the neighbor's lawn, it's not hard to figure out why she's there. There's a grill going and some meat cooking. Any cat named for Joe wouldn't be any place other than where the food is being served.

March 11

DFW to Las Vegas on American Airlines Flight 1417. The land below looks angry, like blistered skin. In places it is puckered and sphincterlike. Ribbons of green grow alongside rivers and creeks, and thin, dark canyons cut snakelike through the land. An occasional small hill protrudes like a solitary breast. Then, a large, snow-covered peak and a scattering of human settlements.

I put on my earplugs so that the banal chatter of the golfers, gamblers, and business consultants is muted. I have a sense of weightlessness, of being suspended as if supported by a benign force. This is an illusion, though. What feels supremely natural is unnatural, as Flight 587 reminds us. I cannot reconcile this feeling of naturalness with the horrible reality of what happened to Joe.

I don't want to stop flying. I want to continue to watch planes take off and land and feel a sense of awe, as I have ever since I was a kid. Long before I met Joe, I was captivated by flight. My father worked for Pratt & Whitney, one of the premiere manufacturers of airplane engines. In our early years together, I was the one who taught Joe the differences between the types of planes. We would sit in the car south of the San Francisco airport and watch the incoming traffic. I taught him how to tell the L-1011 from the DC-10. Later, the roles reversed. Just as he could identify the make and model of every car on the road, Joe knew every airline and airplane. The last thing he taught me was how to distinguish an Airbus A300 from a Boeing 767.

Checking into the Mandalay Bay hotel in Las Vegas, I am reminded of Joe's hotel routine. Check under the beds. Check in the shower. Only then do you lock the door behind you. When you leave the room, put up the "Privacy Please" sign and call out, "See you soon," to the empty room as you leave.

Later that night Lorraine arrives on Southwest from Burbank and we head out for dinner. Mexican food and my first margarita since November 12. Later, we take a few turns at the slots. Lorraine is lucky, winning enough to break even. I quickly go through twenty dollars. After we turn in, I lie awake for a while, hoping to hear Lorraine snore. It's only toward morning that I hear her breathing.

When she wakes up she asks if she was noisy. Only a little, I tell her. Nothing compared to her big brother.

She showers and gets ready, going through her routine in the opulent, oversized bathroom. This is a familiar position for me, waiting for a Lopes to get ready. She's got a lot of equipment, too, including some mysterious tools for her eyebrows and eyelashes. It's worth the wait, though; she looks beautiful. We have breakfast in the hotel, return briefly to the room to collect her bag, and then it's time for her to leave. She needs to be home in time to pick the girls up from school. For each of us, the other is the closest thing we have to Joe now, and we hold each other tightly. Inevitably, though, I have to let her go. She gets into the backseat and the cab pulls away.

I head for the Mandalay Bay Spa where I have a day pass and an appointment for an herbal wrap, whatever that might be. The spa turns out to be a good way to pass the time between conference workshops. I alternate between the pools, the dry sauna, and the steam room. I linger, Joe-like, in front of the mirror in my robe as I shave, apply moisturizer to my face, and run gel through my hair. One of the attendants is particularly friendly and before I leave he asks me if I would like company later on. I hesitate briefly before giving him my room number. I stop at one of the stores off the lobby and, for the first time in my life, purchase condoms. I don't know that I will even need them. Just the thought of safe sex practices and negotiating boundaries and rules is exhausting.

March 13

Big hugs from Aunt Rosemary and Uncle Elliott after I deplane in Tucson. They, Rosemary in particular, were the first among my parents' generation to embrace Joe and welcome him into the family. I can still see the look of delight on her face when they met at Wendy's wedding in 1989. We visited with them twice in Detroit, and twice in Tucson, their winter home.

Our first two days are spent bird watching, and I am able to add six new birds to my life list—a Lincolns' sparrow, a gray flycatcher, a violet-crowned hummingbird, a common ground dove, an Arizona woodpecker, and a burrowing owl. On Saturday morning, eleven of us, including two of my cousins and their families, hike into the desert in Saguaro National Park. It's a spectacular morning. We stop in a dry riverbed by a tall cactus. Rosemary reads a psalm and a poem and my two cousins read and speak about Joe, as do both of their spouses. I say a few words about how Joe was drawn to the desert and how he loved Rosemary and Elliott. I kiss the vase, call out "Stay near," and throw his ashes into the riverbed. There's a gentle wind blowing and it carries some of them upstream. Elliott says this is a good sign. We open a few bottles of sparkling water and have a toast.

Later that night we watch the video of the memorial service. I'm touched that the kids stay through the whole thing. It makes me realize how much laughter occurred during the service. But how could there not be?

Speaking with my cousins and their spouses, I go through "first-time scenarios," reliving the moment when each of them learned about Joe's death. At some point the realization strikes me that I will never lose Joe again. I only have to do that once in life, and I have already survived it. I find some comfort in this.

– XIX –

As a kid, I always rooted for the Indians in the westerns on TV. I was predisposed toward the underdog, but I also thought the Indians were pretty hot. Cary Grant, John Wayne, and Jimmy Stewart did nothing for me. Meanwhile, in Hong Kong, Joe liked to hang around and solicit Chiclets from British and American sailors.

Our first apartment in Manhattan was a half-block west of Charlie Mom's Chinese restaurant. It was our favorite source of take-out dinners. We used to joke that before you could hang up the phone the delivery boy would be at the door. One time, it couldn't have been more than four or five minutes before our buzzer rang. Joe let the delivery boy in, paid him, and put the bag down on the kitchen counter. A few minutes later, I realized that the bag didn't look right. I turned it around and discovered it was from a different restaurant. We looked at the receipt and saw that it was for our next-door neighbor— Apartment 5c instead of 5b. Joe took the bag and knocked on our neighbor's door. Patrick was away and had a guest staying at his apartment. The guest, whom we had never met, opened the door, saw Joe standing there with the food, and assumed he was the delivery boy. "Hold on," he said and went to get the money. He came back, handed Joe the money, said "Thank you," and closed the door. A few minutes later our buzzer rang again with the delivery from Charlie Mom's.

Another time we went out to Woo Lae Oak, the big Korean restaurant in midtown. We were there for the first time without Ben, a Korean friend who had been our guide to his culture's cuisine. We had a hard time understanding the waitress. She had the same problem with us. I told her what I wanted, but it was obvious that she did not get it. I told her a second time and got another blank stare. She looked at Joe. He repeated what I said, word for word, in English. She smiled and her pen leaped into action.

As an Asian, Joe could use certain phrases about other Asians without being politically incorrect. Within our relationships I could use them too. He taught me about "FOB," or "Fresh off the Boat," a term for new immigrants. When we were driving he would occasionally point to a car and call out, "Be careful, DWO." Driving While Oriental. We later expanded it to "DWOSUVNJ." Driving While Oriental in an SUV with New Jersey plates.

We once saw a headline on a tabloid that read, "How Asian Gals Snare American Hubbies." In its own way the headline confirmed that "Rice and Potato" couples, a rarity when Joe and I met, were becoming more common. Joe, of course, was only half rice, but it was his belief that this was how people saw him. Or at least that they saw him as nonwhite. Confusion about which racial minority he belonged to was common, especially when his name was thrown into the mix. The nametag on his uniform read "J. Lopes," and it was not unusual for passengers to ask, "What are you?"

His colleague Tricia told me that she had nicknamed Joe "Chameleon" after an incident with a desk clerk at a hotel. She and Joe had agreed to meet in the lobby and when she realized she was running late she called down to the front desk and asked, "Is there an Asian man waiting in the lobby?" She was told no. There was a Hispanic man, but no Asian man. When she got to the lobby she found Joe standing by the front desk. When told about what the clerk had said, he responded, "I can be Hispanic. I can be Asian."

Once, early in our relationship, my mother asked me over the phone what we would be eating when I told her I was going to Joe's family's house for Thanksgiving dinner. Perhaps she pictured us eating lo mein with chopsticks. Joe got a kick out of this. I laughed, too, but the truth was that when I first met Joe, I valued his ethnicity—all that made him different from me. I would have preferred lo mein to turkey. (The only thing vaguely "ethnic" at his family Thanksgiving was rice—real rice cooked in a rice cooker, not Uncle Ben's.) Ethnicity was cool in the circles I belonged to in San Francisco. I could show Joe off to my friends. The problem was that Joe didn't play along. One of the roommates in my collective household asked him which part of his heritage he most identified with. "Chinese" would have been the correct answer. Instead, he said, "I've always thought of myself as Western." Being attracted to someone on the basis of race was not correct either, but racial stereotypes played a role in our attraction to each other. I was a "rice queen," the name applied to gay men attracted to Asians. Joe was attracted to Caucasians, or, as he liked to put it—English schoolboy types.

Race was only one part of the equation. Within the Chinese side of Joe's inheritance were deep class differences. His father's mother was a domestic servant. His mother's father was from a prominent family, a well-traveled, multilingual university professor. Within his Caucasian side were wide cultural gaps between his German grandmother and his Portuguese grandfather. Then this whole mix of race, culture, and class was uprooted and planted in the middle of the Sunset District of San Francisco which was, at the time, largely Irish. (Joe liked to refer to his youngest brother John, the only one born in the States, as "Sunset Irish.")

Like all stereotypes, that of Asians as the model minority, successfully integrating themselves into Western culture, is only one piece of a more complex reality. When Joe worked at Elmhurst Hospital as a social worker, security guards, clerks, and other employees would greet him with, "Hey, Doc!" An Asian man wearing eyeglasses and a necktie was assumed to be a doctor. He was familiar with the dark side of the Asian success story—resentment by others. On his layovers in European cities, after he shed his uniform, he was not seen as American, but as Asian. Once, in Switzerland, a skinhead pushed him to the ground, leaving him with a minor back injury he never completely recovered from. At home, he was comfortable in New York City, but sometimes on our travels, particularly as we pushed farther into northern New England, he became conscious of what he called "this nonwhite face."

One of the legacies of Joe's multiclass, multiracial, multicultural background was a marvelous facility for language. You never knew what was going to come out of his mouth. Chances were good it would be English, but you never knew what accent it would be delivered in. His mother was fluent in English, German, Cantonese, and Mandarin. Joe grew up speaking English; he spoke Cantonese outside the home until he was ten. As a child he overheard his mother and grandmother speaking German to each other. As an adult, he took classes in German, Mandarin, and Cantonese, although he never went beyond the beginner's level. His gift was not so much for speaking different languages as for the way the languages sounded, for their musicality. What phrases he knew in Mandarin or Cantonese he could throw off like a native speaker, but he could also do on-spot imitations of Chinese speakers trying to speak English. The English he grew up speaking in Hong Kong was British English, and he often imitated a British accent. Joe was good with an Irish brogue as well. He liked to refer to his Sunset Irish brother John as "a big strapping lad."

He picked up on what he heard going on around him. He was adept at black street slang. He regularly employed Spanish-accented English. He knew just enough airplane Spanish to allow him to serve his passengers. *¿Algo a tomar? ¿Jugo de naranja?* There was an irony in his dying on the morning flight to Santo Domingo. One of his favorite work stories was of how matronly Dominican women answered the question as to whether they wanted eggs or pancakes. They usually wanted pancakes, but rather than say what they wanted, they would emphatically tell him what they didn't want. *"¿Huevos o pancakes?"* he would ask. Then, in imitation of a typical response he stuck out his chin, drew down the corners of his mouth in disapproval, waggled his index finger and said, *"No huevos."*

Joe treasured the various accents of New York. He told the story of when a plumber came to our apartment and introduced himself as "dah plummah." He was a surprising source for a convincing "fuhgeddaboudit" or Joey Tribiani's "How you doin'?" from the TV show *Friends.* The Italian-American or Brooklyn accent was the basis for one of his favorite movie lines. In Woody Allen's *Broadway Danny Rose,* Mia Farrow plays a tough-talking Italian-American babe whose boyfriend, Lou Canova, is a washed-up lounge singer. Allen plays his hapless agent. At one point Farrow visits Allen in his run-down midtown apartment and says to him, "Look at you. You're living like a loser" (loo-zah).

The conversion of the words *did you* into *jah* or *djah* and the *er* sound into an *uh* (*her* becomes *huh*) made possible Joe's favorite Three Stooges joke, which his colleague Tricia told at his service:

CURLY: So, did you hear I sent my wife to the West Indies?

MOE: Jamaica?

CURLY: Na, she wanted to go.

Of all the accents Joe employed, none appealed to him more than the classic New York, outer-borough, Jewish accent. His inspiration came first from Woody Allen films, and then the TV show, *The Nanny*. In *Annie Hall,* Alvy Singer, the character played by Allen, recounts a childhood visit to a psychiatrist. In a flashback to 1940s Brooklyn, the young boy sits next to his mother on a couch and morosely lays out what is troubling him. "The universe is expanding . . . Well, the universe is everything and, if it is expanding, someday it will break apart and that will be the end of everything." His mother interrupts him, "What is that your business?" The mother's exasperated question became a stock phrase of Joe's.

He loved the Yiddish tendency to reverse subject and object. "A dollar-fifty the subway costs now." When he began doing it subconsciously, he declared that he had lived in New York too long. When *The Nanny* came along, Joe devoted himself to it. To many, myself included, Fran Drescher's voice was like fingernails on a blackboard, but Joe loved it. He could imitate Fran, her mother, Sylvia, and grandmother Yetta. He could then switch over and do a perfect version of Maxwell, the British theater producer for whom Fran worked, and Niles, the British butler. He loved Fran in the way that he loved Cher. It was outrageous and over the top, and that was exactly the point. Much of the talk between Fran and Sylvia centered on food, and that appealed to Joe. He adopted one of Sylvia's maxims about life as his own: "You'll laugh a little; you'll cry a little; you'll eat a danish."

It was an underlying concern of mine that Joe never really adapted to New York, that given the chance he would prefer to go back to San Francisco. No matter how many times he assured me this was not the case, the fear persisted. I had lunch with his colleague Henri a few months after the crash and he insisted that my fears were groundless. They had flown together in August and Joe kept Henri entertained by doing his favorite Woody Allen moments. "Joe loved New Yorkers," Henri told me. "You can't imitate people that well unless you love them."

Race mattered, and it didn't. It would be naive for me to say that race had no impact on our relationship, but it is difficult to sort out what issues rose out of race, culture, and class, as opposed to personality and temperament. Did our different appraisals of how financially secure we were reflect racial and cultural differences? I came from a family comfortably rooted for generations in the middle-class whereas Joe's family was forced to start from scratch once they reached America. Certainly these contrasting experiences contributed to our differing perceptions of how financially secure our future was. But there was also the issue of temperament. Joe's genius was for the moment; I was better at thinking about the framework of our relationship. He was comfortable right now; I took comfort from the long view.

What is remarkable to me is how much common ground we were able to find. We began with an attraction based on racial stereotypes, but quickly moved beyond that. Thanks to the struggles of an earlier generation, we were able to live openly as an interracial, gay couple. Joe liked to use the phrase "your people" when speaking to me of the British. In San Francisco and then New York, where a new wave of immigration and other progressive forces are redefining and broadening what it means to be an American and to be a family, we found "our" people.

– XX –

March 20

A sad night last night. After my book club meeting I looked at a photo of Joe, Michael, and me that was taken by Stewart along Mink Hollow Road in Woodstock. The picture is not posed; he caught the three of us unaware. Joe is caught in a classic Joe maneuver: both hands are pulling at the bottom of his jacket, straightening it out. He's arranging himself, making sure he looks good. What saddened me was the same thing that makes the picture so appealing—its spontaneity. It was so easy for Joe to be alive then. His heart beat, his lungs drew in air. He could laugh. It took no effort.

An Easter card arrives from Ray Herrman, Joe's best friend from high school. He sends along the picture he used for Joe's obituary in a local paper, the *Bay Area Reporter*. It's a killer. A young Joe looking seductively into the camera. The beautiful square chin is prominent in the picture. Ray writes: "I am very slowly learning to accept Joe's passing. I dressed one of my Barbie [dolls] in a vintage 1963 American Airlines uniform and named her Joe. I hope we all can really be reunited in heaven—I miss Tony and Joe (and my youth)."

March 25

I delete Joe's Juno e-mail account from the laptop at home. I have to enter the password, "sweetpea," to complete the task. I was the one who suggested "sweetpea." I'm now aware of the danger of choosing such sentimental passwords. I have already begun changing "Oliver," which was my most widely used password, to other words. "Are you sure you want to delete the account joelopes@juno.com?" I am asked. Just do it! Just do it! I want to scream at the computer. Then I have to wait until it dials up and connects before it is deleted. I sweep the Juno icon into the recycle bin. The last piece of personal mail Joe received was on the morning of November 12 from George Fossett. It read, Please drop me a line and let me know that you are ok.

March 30

Janet Lopes and her boyfriend, Kevin, arrived last night. I picked them up at JFK, my first trip there since the crash. Janet is our eldest niece. I met her when she was a year-and-a-half old, at her grandmother's funeral. I have always been Uncle Bill to her. Joe had encouraged her to come to New York, but her first visit was for his service. "He was right," she told me. "He always said I would love New York, and I did."

March 31

We drive to Connecticut for Easter dinner at my parents' house. My whole family is there. Even though this is all happening because of Joe's death, it's wonderful to see Janet and Kevin with my family. Kevin is a huge hit with the kids. He has the patience to play endless rounds of softball and kickball.

April 5

Kevin proposes to Janet on a rowboat in Central Park. They appear in the doorway of my office at 5 p.m. and Janet thrusts out her hand at me, showing off her new ring. I'm the first to know. Kudos again to Kevin. He had been planning the whole thing for months, including a trip to Central Park earlier in the week to scout out locations. He managed to sneak the ring into their luggage and through airport security without Janet seeing it. We go out to celebrate with bowling and Japanese food.

April 6

Curbside at JFK, I want to hang on to Janet, but she has to go. Over the years, Joe and I became part of each other's family. Janet's visit confirms that that relationship extends into the next generation.

After leaving JFK, I drive to Jamaica Bay National Wildlife Refuge. Flight 587 flew over Jamaica Bay, leaving its tail in the water before crashing in Far Rockaway. The weather is very strange. Sunny and springlike as I drove to the airport, it snows briefly along the Belt Parkway. By the time I park, it's still cloudy, but rays of sunlight pierce through and shimmer off the bay. I can hear planes overhead.

I am all right. I feel nothing here that I haven't felt elsewhere. I have lost Joe, but I have not lost Jamaica Bay, this world-class birding destination that we visited so often. That is just how he would want it. I walk a bit and get good views of some green-winged teals. I call Michael and record the milestone.

April 9

I have received Joe's tax returns from his accountant. They have "Deceased, Joseph M Lopes, 11/12/01" typed across the top. Joe isn't the deceased type.

Checking pockets in his uniform jacket I find a small card with the names of the crewmembers from Flights 11 and 77.

I take mortgage documents to the co-op office to get them all converted to my name. April 5 was the seventh anniversary of our closing. Of all the paperwork I have had to do, all the stripping off of Joe's name, this one hurts the most. This will always be our home, regardless of what the stock certificates and proprietary lease say.

April 10

From the AviationNow.com Web site:

> . . . aviation accidents in 2001 declined from the previous year across the world, the International Civil Aviation Organization reported Tuesday. . . .

ICAO tracked 13 aircraft accidents in scheduled air services with 577 fatalities in 2001. In 2000, there were 757 fatalities from 18 accidents. The accident rate decreased from 0.025 in 2000 to 0.02 in 2001, using the measurement of passenger fatalities per 100 million passenger kilometers.

– XXI –

April 13

Leaving JFK for Los Angeles on American Airlines Flight 33. The flight departs from the international terminal, the same terminal Flight 587 left from. Looking up at the monitors, I see its replacement, Flight 619. It now departs at 8:30, a half hour later. There will never be another Flight 11, 77, or 587. As we taxi to the runway, a Japan Airlines 747 crosses our path. It may be the same 747 in whose wake Flight 587 became entangled. When I see "JAL" across the fuselage, I can't help but think of Joseph, Anthony, and Lily—the three members of the Lopes family who have been taken from us.

The weather is overcast for takeoff, so I cannot see our exact path, but I believe that we are taking off over Jamaica Bay and the Rockaways. I am calm.

Landing at LAX, another JAL 747 crosses our path as we approach the gate. Lorraine, Nick, and four-year-old Maddy meet me at baggage claim. We drive down to the Irvine Museum, a shrine for California Impressionism.

April 14

Zoe, twelve, is developing into a bird watcher. I'm thrilled to be able to help her along. She has her Uncle Joe's love of animals, but she also seems to have a head for identification and organization, which he never had. It's the perfect combination for a bird watcher. We start working on a trip list and quickly have a dozen birds seen just from the backyard. She is particularly interested in hummingbirds.

A hike through Wildwood Park with Lorraine, Nick, Zoe, and Maddy. Zoe has a pair of opera glasses and we are doing a good job of adding to our list. She's not content to just see the birds; she wants to see the entry in the field guide as well to confirm the identification. A black-headed grosbeak is a great find. Later, I fall behind the family and have some time to myself. I'm thinking about the question of going forward with Joe. How does he come with me? It's still not clear to me. It is clear to me, though, that staying by myself and being afraid to enter into new relationships would *not* be going forward with Joe. That would be clinging on to some unreal image of Joe—as a helpless child needing me to protect him. I still don't know how I could be with someone else and still stay connected to Joe, but I don't face that issue yet. If it ever presents itself, I will face it. And Joe will be with me as I face it.

April 15

Maddy's room is a swirl of toys and clothes. Felix, a huge lump of Australian shepherd, lies in the middle of it. I have brought three Baggies of ashes with me. One is to stay with Lorraine. I hand her the shopping bag and she extracts the ashes.

"Puss is in a Baggie," she says. "Is this all him?"

"I think it is part casket, too. I need to call and find out about that. I found some screws and things in there."

Zoe comes in, Lorraine hands her the ashes. "It's Uncle Joe. That's how we all end up. This is how I want to end up." They discuss where to put the ashes. It's complicated by the fact that they might not stay much longer in this house.

April 16

Lorraine tells Maddy that she can't go outside. Maddy responds, "Yes, I can, Mama. It's my world!" What's startling is that she absolutely believes this. Her mom is constantly saying no to her. She is resilient, though. Seconds after being rebuffed she is back with a new demand, delivered with the absolute conviction that she should and will get her way.

From her car seat she asks, "Uncle Bill, where's Uncle Joe?"

"He's in the sky," I offer.

"Where?"

"In the clouds. He's with God," I say, feeling that I have to give her some kind of answer. I can't think of how to talk about death with children without talking about God, even if I am uncertain of my own beliefs. She doesn't seem to need my explanation, though. "He's right here," she pipes up. I turn around and she is wiggling her fingers. "See, he's right here."

"Good! You keep him right here with us."

April 17

San Francisco. Dinner with Ray Herrman and Gary Greene. Ray is Joe's oldest friend. According to Ray, he and Joe came out in the summer of 1975, when Joe was nineteen. Tony Lopes took them under his wing and showed them the End Up, a gay bar that became known for an East-West connection. Gary met Joe around then. They tell me the story of the Cher concert at a casino at Lake Tahoe. They paid the headwaiter to get a front row table. This was during one of Cher's down times. The audience was not very receptive, except for them. They were so enthusiastic that Cher came over after the show and shook hands with them. Joe and Gary frantically tried to remove their glasses in order to look cooler.

This is one of a handful of stories that define Joe's young adulthood for me. We go through some of the others, like the time Joe was working the counter at the El Rey theater and Sly Stone came and ordered a hot dog. Joe was so nervous, he dropped the hot dog on the floor. Joe and Ray both worked at the theater, Joe as an assistant manager, when it was robbed at gunpoint. Ray also cooked up a scheme for reselling tickets that got them both fired.

April 19

A walk through San Francisco's Castro district, the gay Mecca. At the All American Boy clothing store I buy two T-shirts. In 1979 I went there to outfit myself in one version of the gay uniform at the time—painters' pants and a tank top. I was wearing the painters' pants the night I met Joe at the baths.

Walking around the Castro I think of all of the gay men who have walked these streets in grief because of AIDS. I was relatively untouched by AIDS, but now I walk the same streets, heartbroken. On my way back to the Richmond District I pass the Ralph K. Davies hospital. Tony died there in 1995.

John Lopes tells me that the package I mailed before I left has arrived. He knows it contains Joe's ashes. He asks, "Can I open it up? I just want to let Joe out so that he feels at home."

One of the cups of Joe is divided up so that his siblings all have some to put in their backyards. John plans to put some in the backyard at his dad's house.

I have a brief talk with Ray's mother, Lu, on the phone. "Thank you for being such a good mother to Joe," I tell her. Joe was blessed with many mothers. He adored his own mother and was the favorite of Oma, spending weekends alone with her in her apartment in Hong Kong. Lu adopted him as a teenager, and Joe kept in touch with her all his life through Ray. It's clear to me that I am not the only one who wanted to take care of Joe. He was like a puppy in that sense, bringing out the nurturing instinct in people.

April 20

The fog is just breaking up as we make our way out along the Marin headlands to the Point Bonita Lighthouse. This is my first chance to meet Joe's high school friend Mary Rosinski. Ray and George Fossett are there, as well as Joe's family. Our nephew David has driven up from San Diego to join us. We gather just short of the lighthouse, along a dirt road that hugs the coast. A few feet from the road's edge, the land plunges dramatically to San Francisco Bay. The side of the cliff is covered with spring wildflowers and calla lilies. It's the kind of day that makes people fall instantly in love with San Francisco. It is almost beyond belief that the sky is so blue and the hills so green. Wisps of fog still cling to the towers of the Golden Gate

Bridge. Someone has written a question on one of the benches: "Do you want the short or the long answer?"

I pass the vase with Joe's ashes around so that people can touch him. Lorraine reads a brief letter to Joe. I read Sandburg's poem, "For You." I throw the ashes down the hill. A thin, ghostly vapor hangs briefly in the air before disappearing. We linger, too, until finally the crowd breaks up and heads to Mike and Fran's for lunch.

That night Janet, Kevin, Zoe, and I go bird watching at the San Rafael Sanitary District, then out for bowling and dinner. Despite feeling tired, I am very happy to be doing this. I want to fulfill my responsibilities to my nieces.

April 23

On Sunday I flew back to New York City for a press conference at Lambda Legal Defense Fund to press the case for awarding spousal benefits from the Workers' Compensation system to domestic partners. I returned to California on Monday afternoon and spent the night with Mary Rosinski at her home in Alameda. We are both struck by how odd it is that I am staying at her house without Joe. She said that as she was making the bed up she had this nice feeling that he would like this very much.

Tuesday morning, after Mary leaves for work, I spend some time in her backyard. Although she and Joe hadn't seen each other in more than twenty years, they developed very similar tastes. Her house is decorated in a Mission/Arts and Crafts style, and there are several cats running about, one of whom cozies up to me. Joe would have spent the morning in the backyard under the grapevine designing his own little Alameda bungalow.

I'm thinking about the word *partner*. In the stories I have seen on the Internet about yesterday's press conference, Joe is referred to as my partner. Technically, we were registered Domestic Partners in New York City. Both terms are inadequate. A partnership can be a very temporary relationship. Joe was my *life* partner, no doubt about that. It wasn't just because we were to be together for life, but because of the way our lives were connected. He was my life partner, and yet my life may not even be half over and he is gone.

By lunchtime, I'm in Petaluma, north of San Francisco. This is the home of Vintage Bank Antiques, the source of several fine oil paintings in our apartment. George Fossett has come over to meet me for lunch. I am convinced that George was already a friend of Joe's when I met Joe; he is convinced that Joe and I were already a couple when they met. Either way, George was one of Joe's oldest and dearest friends. They both went through Macy's executive training program. George had a successful career first at Macy's and then later at the Gap. Eventually he dropped out and ended up as a pastry chef in Calistoga.

We have lunch and go through the familiar stories from the past. Joe called George "Georg," in honor of the Christopher Plummer character in *The Sound of Music.* "Oh, dear God! Georg!" was a favorite saying of his. One story of George's used to elicit howls of laughter from Joe. It took place at a market where George and a friend were shopping for produce. The saleswoman asked George, "Does your friend need a bag?" George thought he heard, "Is your friend a fag?"

Later that day I get a call from the flight service manager at JFK. The medical examiner has completed the identification of all remains from Flight 587 and there are additional remains of Joe. As much as I know that Joe was gone by the time his body was destroyed it still hurts to think of it being broken into pieces. The first time I did not ask about the state of his body. I only hoped that it was whole. This time I want to ask. It is always better to know the truth. George offers a comforting shoulder as I process this new information.

I call Lorraine from George's garden to tell her about the new set of ashes. We'll have to do a second round of scatterings. The Ashes Tour—Round 2. We have a good laugh at this.

April 24-26

Wilbur Hot Springs. I have contracted a bad cold, the first time I've gotten sick since November 12. I spend a day lying around doing nothing but reading and sleeping. That night I take a walk along the access road. Cliff swallows flitter above. A scattering of clouds have turned a reddish purple in the sunset. The only sound is that of the river rushing by. I can't resist looking up and asking, "Are you there, Joey?"

I'm tired of having to ask. I'm tired of having to hang any hope of happiness on this thin thread. I call out, "I wish it had been me!" This is the first time I have ever vocalized this wish, and I feel guilty about saying it out loud. I don't even know if it is true. I could never wish this on him. In some ways I think I am better equipped to handle grief than he was.

As I return to the lodge, Valentia, the resident cat, comes toward me. She is strikingly beautiful, black, with a hint of brown, and green eyes. Joe never met her; she is new since our last visit. I sit down and call for her to come so that I can pet her. She refuses. Eventually, though, she comes and sits near me. A lesson, perhaps. I can't just summon up Joe when I see a pretty sunset, yet he may still be close to me, like Valentia.

The next morning I have my own private ash scattering at Wilbur. The morning is cool and I am still fighting a cold. I walk about a mile from the lodge, following a dirt road until I reach a dry creek bed. I turn off the road and follow the creek bed for a few hundred feet to where small pools of water have formed. I have encountered no other human beings on the way out. I set out a towel, Joe's picture, the copper vase with his ashes, and the book of Sandburg poems. I collect a handful of wild flowers and lay them by the vase.

Joe and I first came to Wilbur in November 1980. Joe was very much still grieving the loss of his mother, although he didn't show it. Years later he told me that at one point he went off on his own to have a good sob. Echoing his grief, I burst into loud wails as I sit down. There is no one to hear me, no fear of offending or bothering anyone. I can let the still-raw passions flow, let them spread among the grass-covered hills of Wilbur. I want Wilbur—this ancient repository of geothermal occurrences and human aspirations for healing and health—to know about this particular pain. It can absorb it.

I remove a chunk of bone from the ashes and roll it between my fingers, wondering what part of Joe it is that I am holding. His body, that compact, lithe vehicle in which he moved through this world, was the vessel of the soul that touched so many. I take a minute to celebrate it—its small frame, its slender build, its Eurasian features. Joe was a mix and a blend. His body, like his character, defied easy characterization. I loved his soft brown eyes and dark hair, whether hanging to his shoulders or the buzz cut of his last years. The chin! The chin! And the prominent Adam's apple—perhaps his most masculine parts. These constantly drew the attention of my lips, as did the tip of what he called his "potato" nose. I can still see the swell of his biceps, the gentle curve of his buttocks, the pools and valleys created by the interplay of collarbone, muscle, and tendon. His skin was light brown, darkening in the summer. His body hair was sparsely distributed; enough around the mouth and lips for a modest goatee, the surprisingly thick run of black hair on his lower legs, small tufts on the big toes and under his arms where I was barred entry, a legacy of childhood tickling trauma. The view from behind was lovely as he walked, the lower legs bowed out like parentheses—his dad called them soccer legs—the hips swaying sideways. Even when he walked, he danced.

I loved all this. I can see it so clearly. At times I feel that I can almost still touch and smell him.

In 1980, we arrived late on a Friday night. After registering at the lodge and unloading Joe's car, we drove a quarter-mile down the road to the parking lot. There are no outdoor lights at Wilbur; at night the darkness is profound. Joe clung to my arm as we walked back. It was my first exposure to his mortal fear of snakes. It was also my first experience of how tightly Joe could attach himself to another person and to me in particular. It was a physical attachment, both of his hands clasped tightly around my right arm, but it was symbolic of an emotional attachment as well. The photos we took that weekend are among my favorites. We're both clad in hooded sweatshirts and sweatpants. Joe is in yellow and red; I'm in blue and gray. Our hair extends freely over our ears. Joe's got big floppy bangs. One picture was taken by another guest of the two of us standing with our arms around each other. The camera easily captures the fact that we are very much in love.

We returned to Wilbur the following spring when the hills were green and lush and dotted with the colors of wildflowers. Wilbur was still a hippie outpost in those days and in the large, communal kitchen vegetables and soy products dominated. Joe and I performed a sacrilege one afternoon by cooking hot dogs for lunch. A couple and their young daughter were also in the kitchen. The mother enthusiastically announced that they were having tofu. The little girl, who was perhaps six or seven, hung her head and said with a resigned whine, "I don't like tofu." Joe and I laughed about this all the way home, and the little girl's statement became a permanent phrase in the vocabulary that we as a couple employed only among ourselves. If one of us proposed something that the other was not keen on the other would often mimic the tone of voice of the little girl in the kitchen at Wilbur and say, "I don't like . . ."

It was seventeen years before we returned to Wilbur, which by then had renovated and gentrified. The oil lamps had been replaced by solar-powered lighting. The bathing area was enclosed and lit at night by Arts-and-Crafts-style lanterns. Much of the original charm remained, though. The basic structure of the 1904 lodge was untouched. The waters, the landscape, and the intense sense of solitude and isolation had not been altered. We spent a few nights in both 1998 and 1999 during two-week swings through California. We took no pictures at Wilbur on either trip but, if we had, they would have revealed a couple still very much in love. It was a different kind of love, and for me at least, a much better one. In 1980, other forces were competing for my heart. By 1998, those forces had long since been quelled. I was free to love Joe, and I did. I was by then a bird watcher and much of my time at Wilbur was spent in pursuit of Western birds that I never saw in the East. Joe often accompanied me, especially in 1999 when he had his own set of binoculars. As we walked the roads of Wilbur, I kept both eyes focused upward. Joe split his duties between the sky and road, one eye watching for birds, the other looking down to guard against snakes, lizards, and other reptilian threats.

Now I must perform this private ceremony to honor that part of our life that was just about us. We had our own phrases and gestures. We possessed an encyclopedic knowledge of each other's bodies and witnessed their passages through time, each bemoaning his own decline while trying to assure the other that his body was still a source of pleasure. We shared personal fears and secrets that we kept from others. We exposed our rawest and most vulnerable sides to each other during nightmares, bouts of depression and panic, and fits of anger. We fine-tuned strategies for inflicting pleasure and pain. We cycled through betrayal and forgiveness, estrangement and reconciliation, distance and intimacy. These are part of any long-term, intimate relationship. How we developed them over twenty-one years was unique to us.

They vanished in an instant on November 12 and the void left behind is enormous. Joe will never again reach out his curled pinkie to hook up with mine. Or sneak up behind me, put his nose in my hair, and take a deep sniff. I have memories of these gestures, but the fact that they exist now only in my memory is part of the pain. Before, we shared them. They were a constant reminder, in the same way that a child is, that something—a *we*—had been forged by our union. They belonged to neither individual, but to us. Now it feels as if they are literally imprisoned within my head. I can write about them and tell others about them, but I can never experience them with Joe again. I am one step removed from them. The gestures no longer flow freely between the two of us, living in the world as we did.

What can I say to him in this private moment? How many more times can I tell him that I love him and miss him, attempting to convey in words something that is so deep and pervasive that it ultimately lies beyond the reach of language? I can always rely on Sandburg, as I have so often since November 12, if I fail to find my own words.

Something comes to me, though. I look up and say, "I know I have said many things to you since you died, but have I ever just sat down and said, 'Thank you'?"

To thank another human being, to be truly grateful, is one of the most profound human experiences. I remember choking back tears one night at dinner as I reached my hand across the table toward Joe. It was 1987, close to Thanksgiving. I had been in therapy for a while and found myself in near constant pain. Yet, Joe was there for me. His love had not diminished. I just wanted to tell him how thankful I was for his presence. It took a long time to get the words out. He got up out of his chair and came and put his arms around me as I worked at it.

The words "thank" and "you" are only sounds. Reaching my hand across the table and Joe holding me in his arms are physical gestures. What about the emotions behind the words and gestures and the longings they represent? They are what matter. Are they bound by the body? Do they exist after a body is extinguished? Is Joe aware of my gratitude even though the eardrums through which he could hear my words and the eyes through which he could see my tears are now ashes?

I don't know. We don't know; we are bound by our bodies. I stand up and take the copper vase to the streambed. I sprinkle some ashes over the grass and wildflowers, and some in the pool of water. It is my hope that when the rains come the streambed will fill and a fragment of ash will be carried to the river where it will make its way to the baths at Wilbur Hot Springs. Some day next winter a lucky bather, without knowing it, will be touched by Joe Lopes.

April 27

One final visit in California, to another of Joe's "mothers." Joe always spoke so warmly of Mary Rosinski's parents and of how they welcomed him into their family and home. It is a classic San Francisco home, high up on Twin Peaks with drop-dead views of the Golden Gate Bridge and the Marin headlands. As Jeanne takes me on a tour, I linger in front of one of the north-facing windows. I can imagine Joe doing the same thirty years earlier. It may have been one of his very first "Can-We-Take-a-Minute" Zen moments.

April 28

Things of Joe's left behind in California: Abraham Lincoln High School yearbooks and two scarves with Mary. A collection of 45s and assorted family pictures with Lorraine. Various stuffed animals and airline trinkets with Zoe and Maddy.

As I depart, John Lopes, that "big strapping lad," stands in the doorway in the predawn darkness and watches over me until the car pulls away from the curve.

American Airlines Flight 182 from San Francisco to JFK. The crew spoils me. They offer me a ride into Manhattan on the crew van. One of the benefits of being an airline spouse was having access to certain things that the general public doesn't. Joe could park for free at the employee parking lot at JFK and we rode the employee bus back and forth to the terminal. If our flight was delayed, we could wait in the operations center. I never rode in a crew van with Joe, though. Two of the women are talking about buying underwear. One says she doesn't wear a bra; the other doesn't wear panties. They say they should team up together for shopping. I have a feeling Joe would have been right in the middle of this conversation.

– XXII –

May 2

A trip to the Morningside Gardens management office to sign the new proprietary lease and stock certificates, which have been reissued in my name only. To make the event even more depressing, it's cold and raining. On the way, a bird catches my eye. I assume it's a house sparrow, but on further inspection it turns out to be a hermit thrush. It's a very elegant bird with a cinnamon-colored back and a reddish tail. The white breast is streaked with brown. It may have been Joe's favorite bird, in part because it is relatively easy to see, poking around on the ground a lot.

May 10

A fax of the release receipt from the medical examiner's office indicates that on 11/19/02 partial remains of Joseph Lopes were released. I give up on the idea that it is better to know the truth about Joe's body. The only way to find out now would be to call the medical examiner's office and ask what pieces of Joe were in the first delivery and what pieces were in the second. It's unlikely that they would even know. Would they have kept a list? Even if they did, do I really want to hear someone read that list to me over the phone?

It would be comforting to think that Joe's body was whole, but it obviously wasn't. One fear is that other bodies were, but his body was somehow singled out for punishment and broken up. I know this is not true; the letter from the medical examiner stated that 2,070 remains were identified, but the fear lingers.

May 12

Mother's Day. Might Joe be with his beloved Lily for first time in twenty-two years? I have a talk with him and tell him how much it feels like he is here. Last night, the apartment was so much a reflection of him. The way I talk, feel, express emotion, my daily routines—all of these were developed with him. I can't separate what was me from what became me with Joe. He is here because he is so much a part of me.

Today is the six-month anniversary of the crash of Flight 587.

May 13

A vivid dream just before I wake up. I am supposed to carry some kind of material that is dangerous or radioactive. Several San Francisco fire trucks are nearby. Then I am in a room with a group of people. A boy in the back of the room keeps talking. I tell him to be quiet several times before he shuts up. I turn around and Joe is there. I have a close-up of his face from the side. It is radiant. He looks so beautiful.

It's interesting that I have this dream at the six-month anniversary. Yes, I have been given a big burden to carry. I am not alone, though, as evidenced by the fire trucks—representative of Joe's family and his two brothers, Rick and John, who are San Francisco firemen.

John Lopes leaves a message that he took some of Joe's ashes out to Colma, where Lily, Oma, and Granny are buried. John visits them every Mother's Day.

Junk mail for Joe: A flyer for a conference called "Advanced Bereavement Facilitator, Certificate Award Program." Topics include "Cutting-Edge Theory and Practice in Bereavement Work" and "A New Diagnostic Category—Traumatic Grief."

May 14

Ollie is delivered to the Hypurrcat facility in northern Westchester County. It's dedicated to the treatment of hyperthyroidism in cats. He will be given a shot of radioactive iodine, and then spend a week in isolation as the radioactive matter works its way out of his system. He has his own private cage, piped-in music and birdcalls, and a cage of finches to keep him occupied. The best part is that there is a Web cam so that I can monitor him throughout his stay. I send the Web address around in an e-mail so that others can watch him, too. Ollie Lopes-Valentine, international Web star.

May 16

Saying the Serenity Prayer at Joe's urn in the morning: "God grant me the serenity to accept the things I cannot change. The courage to change me. . . ." I have a good laugh at this. I don't want to change too much. I don't believe we can change much of what is essential about ourselves.

May 17-19

Cape May, New Jersey
New Jersey Audubon Society Spring Weekend

I'm here for my first pelagic birding experience—birding from a boat. The big question is, can I bird without barfing? Before boarding, I go through all of the various preparations people had recommended to me: two antihistamine tablets first thing in the morning, one Dramamine with lunch an hour before launch time, special wristbands, and a pack of crackers onboard with me. The trip is four hours—two hours out and two hours back. A strong chop is evident as we head out into Delaware Bay on our way to the Atlantic. Once we clear shore the chop dies down, but a strong swell persists with intense up-and-down rocking. Because the winds have been westerly for the past few days, very few birds are present. All I can do is think about my fragile stomach and wonder if it is going to make it. It's doing fine, though. Not even a hint of queasiness. After four hours I step off the boat and onto the dock without having seen a single new bird on the trip, but I gained something more important. I've learned I can bird by boat.

On the boat I happened to sit next to a gay couple from New York.
I seek them out in the large banquet hall when I go for dinner on Friday night. There are more than five hundred people, though, so after
a few minutes I give up and take an empty seat at one of the tables. I
introduce myself to my tablemates and we discuss the topic at hand—
birding. At one point, I turn around and look at the table behind me.
To my surprise I see the couple from New York, an empty seat next to
them. I get up and ask them if the seat is available. It is, and they ask
me to join them. Excusing myself from my table, I take my soup and
move to their table. They are sitting with three others—a man and a
woman who live in Hong Kong and a woman who used to live in
Hong Kong but now lives in New York. The Cape May festival has
attracted birders from around the country, but the couple from Hong
Kong win the prize for the longest distance traveled. I can't help but
notice that they are a rice and potato couple. The woman is Chinese
and the man is Australian, and a redhead to boot.

Saturday dawns cold and raining. Between field trips I have lunch
by myself in a diner. For some reason I send myself back into the last
moments of Flight 587. How bad was it? How long did Joe know that
he was going to die? It is surreal to try to put myself into that frame of
mind, to go from sitting in a diner eating crab cakes to a doomed
plane falling to the ground. I hold it together until I get outside. In
the car, I say out loud, "I'm sorry. I'm so sorry you had to go through
that. I know you must have been terrified. I wish I could have protected you." I also say, "I don't want to die, but I don't feel afraid of it
anymore. All death means now is that whatever happened to you will
happen to me. That's a gift you gave me."

That night at dinner I again seek out the couple from New York.
I find them easily this time. They're with the same three people and I
take the empty chair. The Chinese woman has brought cards with
stickers of birds native to Hong Kong and she gives me a packet. I
wish Joe were here to see these. He would have loved to see birds from
his native land. I'm sitting on one side of the couple from Manhattan
and the woman who used to live in Hong Kong but now lives in New
York is on the other side. The topic of conversation works its way
around to hunting and its use as a means of controlling populations of

deer and Canada geese. John, sitting next to me, opposes it. The woman thinks it can be humane if done correctly. "Live well, die quickly," is her credo. She repeats it several times during the course of the conversation.

It's interesting that I should hear this just a few hours after having agonized over Joe's last moments. He lived well and died quickly—although I am certain he felt terror before he died. It was not a bullet to the brain. The conversation moves on and, inevitably, turns to September 11. The woman from New York lives in Far Rockaway and she tells of how she was driving into Manhattan that morning and saw the second plane hit the south tower. John recounts a friend's experience leaving an office on Duane Street through a shower of debris and body parts. I don't want to hear this. It was just within the last week that I learned definitively that Joe's body was fragmented. I'm leaning back in my chair, away from the conversation, trying to direct my attention elsewhere when I hear the woman say, "And then there was Flight 587. I was at home and saw it crash."

It's not until she says this that it fully sinks in how strange this encounter is. I'm sitting in a hotel in Cape May, New Jersey, and I have people from Hong Kong, where Joe was born, and from Far Rockaway, where he died, sitting across the table from me. What's even more interesting is that Hong Kong is represented by a couple—a rice and red-headed potato couple—while Rockaway is represented by one person. Joe's birth in Hong Kong led to our coupling. His death in Rockaway led to my being single.

This whole encounter again raises the question of just how alone I am. It remains a question for me; I find no certainties in it. But because the question continually reasserts itself in surprising and interesting ways is in itself a partial answer. No specific coincidence provides proof of Joe's eternal life, but the string of coincidences I have experienced makes me hopeful that a spirit world in which the dead maintain a connection to the living does exist.

It feels like this encounter completes some kind of framework. Perhaps the combination of six months, my first trip by myself, and this strange encounter are the impetus for declaring that something has changed. It is not that the grief has ended; it never will. The pain is not gone, as I have learned several times this weekend. I still love and miss Joe Lopes, and always will. Yet it is also important to recognize that as surely as our physical relationship ended, so too has this period of full-time grief. Joe's absence does not weigh on me as much. It is balanced by his presence as captured in memories, but even more important, in my recognition that who I am today is very much a reflection of who Joe Lopes was.

– XXIII –

May 21

The funeral home is out of urns, and this is holding up the second batch of Joe's ashes. I tell them I'll pick them up in whatever they came in. I don't want another object to which I will feel committed. I'm already resentful of the first urn and the power it has over me. I can't walk into the living room without feeling that I have to greet it. If I go for too long without sitting down in front of it and talking, I feel that I am ignoring Joe.

E-mail from Lorraine regarding my experience in Cape May:

The hardest thing for me about dying is the fear involved. I have a favorite prayer to Tony and Joe and Mom, and that's "teach me to die without fear." I know Joe experienced fear, as did Tony and Mom (I remember seeing Mom crying by the sink once as she did the dishes). But I'm assuming we all go through it. There's fear in birth as well, I'm sure. I just don't know why we die the deaths we do. With a terminal illness you can finally let the death go—I don't know if I will ever get over Joe dying the way he did.

I think she is right and I'm sure that when my time comes I will be afraid. Just not as much as before, and that's still a gift. I think she is right also in that Joe's death is particularly hard to get over. I am moving on; we all are. We have little choice. We can dig in our heels, but we are all hurtling forward. I still relive the shock over and over, whether it be the moment I heard it on the radio, or thinking about all the individual moments when others heard it, or thinking about Joe himself. It is still such a gut-wrenching experience to think about that.

May 2

I retrieve Ollie from his luxury digs in Westchester. He looks fine. Loretta sniffs his butt to welcome him home. I go and sit by Joe's urn so that he will come over and rub up against it.

After work I pick up Joe. A man is sitting at a desk talking on the phone as I walk in. "Can I help you?" he asks.

"I'm here to pick up some remains."

He hurries to finish his conversation on the phone. It sounds like he's been arguing with his wife. "Whose?"

"Joseph Lopes."

On the floor in the corner of the office are several small cardboard boxes. He picks up one of the small ones and brings it to the desk. I'm immediately relieved that the box is small. This means that the first time we got most of Joe.

I fill out the paperwork. He asks, "You understand how this works?"

The situation is a little out of the ordinary in that the ashes are not in an urn. "Yes," I respond. "This is my second round."

"Yeah, unfortunately, huh?" He looks up at me sympathetically. I sign a form and start to leave. He asks, "Do you want a bag?"

"Sure, why not?"

He rummages around for a bag and finds a nice, white paper shopping bag, like the kind you'd get at Williams-Sonoma or some other upscale store. This is just going to be a plain bag, right? No. On the side of the bag, in green lettering, it says, "Walter B. Cooke Funeral Home." Off I go, down East 87th Street and into the subway with my Walter B. Cooke shopping bag. The emblem is facing out so everyone can see it. When I get home, I mix the ashes in with the old ones. The new ones are a slightly different color, which is odd. I take this to mean that the ashes themselves are composed mainly of the container. I see bone chips, so I feel that we have some of Joe.

It's a beautiful night, one of those warm spring evenings that I feared so much in the winter. I call Michael to report in and leave a message for Lorraine. I take the urn out onto the porch, pour myself a drink, and watch the sunset over the Palisades of New Jersey.

May 24

Today is the seventh anniversary of our moving into Morningside Gardens.

The urn is now in the back room. I am slowly detaching from it as the object through which I connect to Joe. The detachment started after I returned from California. I began giving myself permission to leave the apartment in the morning and to go to bed at night without stopping by the urn.

After dinner, I detour to my closet and take out a cheap, Hawaiian-style shirt. Impulsively, I decide to throw it out. Getting rid of a shirt of my own gives me the courage to grab some of Joe's uniform shirts hanging in his closet. I have been aware for some time that when it came to Joe's clothes, the uniform was going to present a special problem. He looked so good in it. That's not the problem, though; it's that his uniform could be used by terrorists. I don't feel comfortable putting it into circulation. It will have to be thrown away. I remove all of his work shirts from the closet, at least a dozen, all with an American Airlines label inside. I carefully fold each. In various closets I find two sets of jackets and pants, a special serving jacket, two AA sweaters, and, finally, three ties, all still impeccably knotted. Everything goes in a large garbage bag. My one shirt seems insufficient to accompany such important cargo, so I take Dumbo, a stuffed elephant that I have had since I was born, and put him in the bag, too. I let it sit overnight in case I want to change my mind. In the morning, though, my resolve is still present. On the way out of town I drop it off in the trash area in the basement. When I come back on Sunday, the bag is gone.

As I remove things from his closet, I am moving some of my own things in. What I fear is coming into the room and seeing his closet empty.

May 25

Memorial Day weekend. The Joe Lopes Spool Collection (used as candleholders) and the Joe Lopes Cookbook Collection (consisting of three books from which, to the best of my recollection, he never cooked me a single meal) both come with me to Chris Lopes's and Autumn's home in Chester County, Pennsylvania. I bring ashes for them as well. They have bought a "Joe" bench. It is set up in the backyard, overlooking the garden.

May 26

Today is the seventh anniversary of Tony Lopes' death. Joe was not only blessed with many mothers, he had a gay older brother to shepherd him through the coming-out process. When Tony told his parents he was gay, he told them about Joe as well. I never got a full report of the conversation, but I always had a picture of Tony talking with his parents and then saying at the end, "Oh, I almost forgot. Joe, too."

Tony was the second son, born February 5, 1953, in Hong Kong. He graduated from Lowell, San Francisco's most academically rigorous high school, but was largely self-educated beyond that. He spent most of his working life in the Art and Music Department of the San Francisco Public Library. He was a voracious reader and thinker. His conversations were sprinkled with references to philosophy, literature, and cultural criticism. His meaning often eluded me, though; at times it felt as if he used words to erect a wall around himself. He wrote in his journal, "I think in an ongoing, unceasing ebb and flow of sensation rising to thought and articulation. It is a deep consolation." Consoling for him, perhaps, but less so for a listener. Once I called Tony and he took off on a long monologue and nearly hung up before I reminded him that I had called him and had business to discuss.

He was a bundle of contradictions. Defiantly gay, he was also the dutiful Chinese son who moved back home for twelve years following his mother's death to raise John and care for his father (whose conservative Catholic faith foretold eternal damnation for the son on whom he was now dependent). Scornful of the nuclear family and bourgeois society, he doted on his nieces and nephews and was a loving and protective older brother to Lorraine. Passionate about art and music, he never visited us in New York despite being able to fly for free on Joe's passes. He was proud that Joe and I built a long-term relationship

("Dear Mr. and Mrs. Joe and Bill, I think it's just faboo how well you two have thrived together," he wrote us in 1994), yet he failed to attend the tenth anniversary celebration we threw in San Francisco.

I did not know Tony well—I found it impossible to get to know him—but he struck me as someone who was not at home in the world. Then he began to die from AIDS. He decided to do so consciously, fully aware of the process he was undergoing. In so doing, he seemed to have found a reason to live. When Joe and I said good-bye to him in October 1994, he appeared to me to have achieved a Zen-like state. Shriveled and wrinkled, as gaunt as a ghost, he spent the weekend conducting a seminar for his family in living well through dying. Even his death seven months later appeared from a distance to be peaceful. He was not hospitalized until a few days before his death. It seemed that he slipped away gently.

It was only after reading his journal that I saw how incomplete, and perhaps naive, my view of his dying had been. Although he did achieve a certain equanimity in his final months, dying was a long, often torturous process for him. Joe and I were, to some extent, leading post-AIDS lives. We were both HIV negative, as were most of our friends. Tony's life, with the exception of interactions with his family, was given over to AIDS. He lived in a world populated by the dying. He never suffered an illness that required a hospital stay, but the decline of his body was prolonged, messy, and painful.

He titled the journal *Eye on the Rear View*, the suggestive pun certainly intended. Much of it is written in staccato bursts, randomly placed side by side without any readily apparent connection. At times the journal seems to be nothing more than a showcase for his erudition. He throws off quote after quote from Italo Calvino, Octavio Paz, Wallace Stevens, Annie Dillard, Wright Morris, T. S. Eliot, and most extensively, Camille Paglia and Michele Foucault. From time to time, though, Tony emerges, and when he does it is often in prose that is both refreshingly direct and poignant.

He dedicated the journal to his mother and to "the ones who came into the family," including me. He then added that he hoped a copy would be given to each of his nieces and nephews when they turn twenty-five, "whether their parents approve or not."

A few of his final entries:

11/11/94

Life is stupid beyond belief. You spend it trying to avoid death. And then when you realize it's inevitable it takes forever to get here.

Later: I have always dreaded this the most: needing to come home to die. I was hoping to spare everyone, to fastforward to the end. But I'm beginning to be glad not to have things my way. It's good being home . . . Even the level of pain seems to have gone down these last few days.

11/22/94

The Angel of Death is an incompetent twit. Why am I still here? (Serves me right, I suppose, for always being late myself. Besides, I'll be the late Tony Lopes soon enough.)

Had a frightening night . . . I woke up totally disoriented and I stumbled into the kitchen to find something to eat. As usual, the house was arctic. (I must remind dad to stop turning the thermostat down.) Anyway, I shit in my pants twice tonight.

Thank God John finally got home from school. Because I was miserable and fucking helpless and getting a chance to talk to him was such a relief. He's so sweet and I'm so grateful to have been a part of his life.

It's so quiet here at Dad's. When I open the bedroom window to blow my cigarette smoke out—as if in high school—I can hear the ocean and fog horns.

1/1/95

New Year's Day

The analgesic power of love: I woke up raw and in much pain. Then Mike and Fran came over this afternoon with the kids.

They stayed late tonight. Fran outdid herself with a perfect leg of lamb, chicken, potatoes and yams. French cut green beans with mushrooms and gravy.

John finally got notice to report to work on January 17th [to the San Francisco Fire Department]. The family is elated. Now I can die, I think. I feel mortal. But also very vibrant.

5/11/95

Finally. Mercifully. It is confirmed by my nurse from HomeCare that I might be released from this poor bag of blood and bones soon.

5/12/95

Musings and amusings. I'd like to be around for some tiramisu next Saturday in celebration of John's and Janet's birthdays . . . And then universe take me home please.

5/21/95

John's birthday

No respite from the rectal bleeding. Lately it is much more profane and painful. Congealed clumps of it.

Despite the glories of music nothing approaches the beauty of birdsong.

That was Tony's last entry. A few days later he was admitted to the hospice at Davies Medical Center. Fran reported that he was calm and in a state of childlike wonder as he looked about his chosen place of death. On May 26, John came to visit. He sat by Tony's bed and told him how much it meant to him that he had devoted so much of his life to raising him. He went out for a cigarette and when he came back he learned that Tony had died. It was 1:50 in the afternoon.

Lorraine made a final entry in the journal, noting Tony's death and adding an excerpt from a poem he had shown her recently:

> Suddenly I realized
> That if I stepped out of my body I would break
> Into blossom.
>
> James Wright, "A Blessing"

Like the final images of his journal—congealed clumps of rectal bleeding and birdsong—the poem offers contrasting symbols of death and rebirth, of breaking and blossoming. It comes as close as is humanly possible to describing the complex and contradictory reality that was the earthly existence of Tony Lopes.

With little experience in death, I kept wondering how we would get through that moment when we learned of Tony's end, as if time would stand still until we figured out what to do. I was out for a run when Lorraine called with the news. When I came home I found Joe sitting on the couch. I sat with him and held him as he cried. His first words were, "I'm so glad that I have you." Eventually, we stood up and went about our lives. Joe made plans to fly to San Francisco. We decided that I would stay behind and keep working on our new home.

At some point Joe received a copy of Tony's journal. It had been typed up by Ray Herrman and distributed by Lorraine. He started to read it, and then put it aside. I'm sure he found it too thick and abstract. Perhaps he was also unsettled by the anger underlying the early parts. I found the journal in his papers after he died. It was open to the page he left off on, about a quarter of the way through. I wish he had made it to the end, where a more humane view of Tony emerges. I regret that he did not make it at least to the entry on June

30, 1993, a quote from the blues singer Bessie Smith. "You've been a good ole wagon, daddy, but you done broke down." Her line surely would have become a part of our vocabulary, chronicling our descent into middle age.

– XXIV –

June 1

Sarah is appointed curator of the Joe Lopes Cat Book Collection.
Lorraine is appointed curator of the Joe Lopes Chinese Literature
Collection. An excerpt from the letter I wrote to accompany the col-
lection:

> Nien Cheng's *Life and Death in Shanghai* was the first book by
> a Chinese author that I recall Joe reading. I'm sure your family
> history and the fact that your mother was a Cheng had some-
> thing to do with his loving it so much. He was drawn to stories
> by strong women such as Cheng and Bette Bao Lord.
>
> Joe was not a big reader when I met him; he was much more
> of a TV guy. He had to read Gerald Durrell's *My Family and
> Other Animals* in college and that book turned him on to reading.
> He also mentioned J.D. Salinger, particularly *Franny and Zooey,*
> as being very important to him.
>
> When we discovered Armistead Maupin's *Tales of the City,* he
> devoured the whole series. The first long book he took on was
> Larry McMurtry's *Lonesome Dove.* I remember sitting on the
> couch on Morton Street and hearing him say from the bedroom,
> "I can't believe that I'm reading a book that is nine hundred
> forty-five pages long." He was very proud to finish that book. I
> think it marked a kind of turning point for him. He remained a
> TV/movie person to the end, but reading seemed to take a much
> bigger role in his life after that. He always took a book with him
> on his flights.
>
> He developed a love of British literature, fed, no doubt, by his
> visits to London. He read all of Jane Austen and quite a bit of the
> Brontë sisters. He loved the richness and formality of the lan-

guage in these books. Every once in a while, he would put one of the books down and say to me, "Oh, William. Your people!" Rudyard Kipling's *The Jungle Book* perished with him on Flight 587. An interesting choice, given the war that was raging in Afghanistan at the time.

We went to the Steinbeck Museum in Salinas, California, in October 2000 and he bought *Travels with Charley*. I read it recently, and can just imagine how much Joe enjoyed it. The language is clear and direct and the dog, Charley, is as fully a developed character as any human could be. Finally, he loved Harry Potter. He just loved him. The other day I took volume four off the shelf to lend to Michael and discovered that the flap was tucked into page ten. I wish he had gotten to finish it.

The curator of the Joe Lopes Adult Video Collection will remain anonymous.

I pack up a large box of clothes to send to Rick. He is the brother closest in size to Joe. I want him to have Joe's wool overcoat. Joe looked great in it and somewhere in the local CBS affiliate's archives is a brief clip of Joe wearing it. He was interviewed outside the Ziegfeld Theater after a showing of the movie *Primary Colors*. The coat only takes up a fraction of the box, so I add in a suit, some shoes, and a few pairs of pants. Then I begin to sort through his sweaters and knit tops. Before I pack them away I unfold and refold them. I fear that all evidence of his brilliant system of folding is disappearing; these tops might be the last items he folded personally. As I unravel each one, I take note of the location of the fold lines. It is from these well-worn creases that I must extract the logic of his system. Each shirt looks perfect as I put it in the box. I've gained some new tips, but it is still a question in my mind as to whether I will be able to replicate his handiwork without his folds to guide me.

His folding system is not the only thing that is disappearing. His handwriting is going, too. The videotape that we used for years to tape TV shows has finally given out. I threw it away, but not before trying to save the label first, which Joe wrote. His handwriting is preserved in letters, cards, and many other places, but these are all filed away. One place where his handwriting is preserved in the open is on the container that holds toys and brushes for the cats. The label reads, "Our Favorite Things."

June 6

Joe's albums are now out of the closet, about ninety in all. They lie in piles on the floor in the back room, except for Cher and Barbra Streisand. These two collections have already been shipped out to their respective curators, Gary Greene for Cher and George Fossett for Babs.

I knew from the beginning that along with his clothes, Joe's albums would be the hardest to deal with. They were like old friends of his, each bringing with it a set of memories and emotions. He carted these albums around to five different apartments in San Francisco, shipped them off to Chicago, and brought them to New York in 1984. They went with us from Brooklyn to Jackson Heights, to Westchester, to Greenwich Village, to Riverside Drive, and finally to Morningside Gardens. At times I tried to dislodge them from Joe's grip, but I never came close—unless there was a case in which we had purchased a CD of the album. Even when our turntable gave out two years ago, Joe steadfastly refused to get rid of his albums, or even winnow them down. He kept insisting that he would get the turntable repaired.

Here, then, is an accounting of Joe's albums at the time of his death. Almost all of them had been collected by the time I met him, or shortly thereafter:

Rock & Roll and its various offshoots acceptable to the kind of suburban white boys I grew up around: Chicago, Mark-Almond, Bonnie Raitt,

Janis Joplin, Simon & Garfunkel, Elton John, Hall & Oates, James Taylor, Steely Dan, The Beatles, The Eagles, The Beach Boys, Doobie Brothers, Michael Franks, Boz Scaggs, Stray Cats

R & B/Soul: Quincy Jones, Stevie Wonder, Michael Jackson, Jackson 5, Chubby Checker

Country: Willie Nelson, John Denver's Christmas album

Disco & other gay-friendly groups: Donna Summer, Melba Moore, Culture Club, Blondie

Classical: Tchaikovsky, Pachelbel, Johann Strauss

White Female Vocalists: Melissa Manchester, Janis Ian, Bette Middler, Carly Simon, Cher, Barbra Streisand, Maria Muldaur, Connie Francis

Jazz & Swing: George Benson, Charlie Byrd, Tommy Dorsey, Louis Armstrong, Gilberto & Jobim, Spyro Gyra

Military/March: Sousa's Greatest Marches (Henry Mancini)

Black Female Vocalists: Diana Ross & the Supremes, Dionne Warwick, The Pointer Sisters, Grace Jones

Vocal Groups: The Lettermen, Manhattan Transfer, The Platters, Mills Brothers

Male Vocalists: Frankie Valli, Tony Bennett, Nat King Cole, Frank Sinatra

Soundtracks: South Pacific, The Turning Point, Foxes, Grease, Cabaret

Anthologies: The Motown Story, The Big Band Sound of the Thirties, A Night at Studio 54

Brazilian: Deodato, Walter Wanderley (Brazil's no. 1 organist), Sergio Mendes & Brasil '66

Home-Grown, Bay Area favorites: Faye Carol, Sly and the Family Stone

The album that foreshadowed our union: Allman and Woman (Gregg Allman & Cher)

Against stereotype, there is no opera and only one Broadway show. It's a pretty sophisticated collection considering Joe was in his teens and early twenties when he put it together. It's also striking in its variety. In that sense, it's a good reflection of Joe. He could stretch to incorporate Tchaikovsky and Donna Summer, Boz Scaggs and Connie Francis, Barbra Streisand and the Doobie Brothers, Melba Moore and John Philip Sousa.

I owned very little music in my early life; I did not need a personal music collection readily at hand. I listened to FM radio, and to what others had. The few albums I owned were typical suburban-white-boy albums: The Doors, Ten Years After, Jesse Colin Young, and Hot Tuna. I branched out into bluegrass via Doc Watson and the blues via Roy Buchanan. I did have one album that pointed in the musical direction in which Joe would take me: Mahalia Jackson. He also had one that pointed in the direction I would take him: *Brothers and Sisters* by the Allman Brothers Band.

When we began to build our own collection Joe specialized in female vocalists—Billie Holiday, Ella Fitzgerald, Sarah Vaughan, Shirley Horn, Peggy Lee, Jo Stafford, Diana Krall; Etta James. I added in classical pieces (what we called "Sunday morning music"), the Allman Brothers, and jazz instrumentalists such as Miles Davis, Coleman Hawkins, Oscar Peterson, Lester Young, and Clifford Brown. John Coltrane and Charlie Parker were as far as we were willing to stray from melody. It is a good collection, but I feel uncertain about its direction. I'm reluctant to take on sole stewardship of something that was so much Joe's, initially, and then ours.

– XXV –

June 4

I am more accepting of the fact that Joe experienced fear, and perhaps terror, before he died. How could he not have? A colleague of mine who lost her husband to a sudden heart attack tells me that as time passes you have a longer view, encompassing the whole relationship, but there remains a primordial part of the brain that always focuses on the moment of death.

Part of me selfishly wishes that, if Joe had to die, he had had a prolonged death, like Tony's. Then we could have talked it through and had a chance to say good-bye. The wish is motivated by a fantasy: that we could have tied up all our loose ends and worked out all our issues. I am thinking again of Joe's fear that I would leave him for a younger man. It does not constitute a failure of the relationship. The strength of our relationship lay not in the absence of issues, but in the commitment we both shared to working through them over time.

June 14

A few of Joe's personal items have been retrieved from the crash site. They are pieces of various cards: AAA, UnitedHealthcare, Bell Atlantic, and appointment cards from our dentist and veterinarian. None of the cards are whole; they have been cut up to remove the charred portions. There is one item that it is not damaged, a plastic access card, the kind used in hotel doors. It says JFK 3824 on it. I imagine it was used for access to a secure area, perhaps the jet bridge. It's curious why this is undamaged. And how did they know it was Joe's, since there is no name on it? Is it possible that it was on his person, and yet not burned? The whole thing is curious. The other cards would have been in a wallet, yet no wallet was returned.

The cards are representative of the security and comforts that middle-class Americans take for granted. AAA, for round the clock roadside assistance; UnitedHealthcare, for cradle-to-grave health care; Bell Atlantic (now Verizon) for instantaneous, worldwide communication. Yet Joe was beyond rescue. Even the most sophisticated medical technologies could not revive his body. At the moment of maximum peril, he had no way to communicate with any of us.

The access card granted him access to a secure area, where he ultimately died. That it is the only card that survived whole and unblemished would seem to mock our belief that the world can be made safe and secure. That is the view from here, anyway. Another view would be that the clean, white card is a symbol left behind to indicate that Joe really did get to a secure place. At one end of the card is a triangle with the words, "Insert Here." When you hold the card up like you would just before you use it, the triangle faces skyward.

June 17

NYU has granted me a two-month unpaid leave of absence. On the first morning, just as I start writing, Ollie comes in and leaves a present in the litter box of such potency that I have to get up and flush it so that I can continue. A few hours later he returns and leaves another present. This one is not quite as potent and I am able to continue working for a while before scooping. In my mind, I can hear Joe's frequent question, "Ollie, didn't your mama teach you to cover up your business?"

A new kind of cat food is supposed to help manage fur balls. My hope was that it would cut down on his vomiting, but after just a few days, he throws up five times in one morning. Ollie is an eating, drinking, pissing, shitting, shedding, vomiting, whining machine. He is also a love machine, which is why he is still here.

Fireflies are visible on the grounds at Morningside Gardens at night now. Joe and I both loved living in a place in the city where fireflies illuminate the paths and small children with glass jars chase after them.

June 26

My thinking continues to evolve about Joe's "I'm afraid you'll leave me for a younger man" remark. Initially, it tormented me. I was afraid that he left this world unaware of how much I loved him and how committed to our future I was. Another view has emerged now, one that sees the comment as a blessing. It showed me that Joe had issues, too. He was having a hard time growing old. There were many other indications. He had two moles removed from his face, he was saving up for braces, and he obsessed about hair coloring. For so long my issues had dominated our relationship, and now it was time to turn our attention to one of Joe's. That we did not have the opportunity to work through this is a source of great sadness to me. But the fact that he alerted me to it just before he died comforts me. The tendency is to make a saint of Joe and enshrine his love for me as selfless and uncomplicated. In truth, our relationship was always a work in progress, continually evolving through ups and downs. By showing me his fears, he was showing me that we both loved imperfectly, which is to say, humanly.

July 4

Grayling, Michigan. The Kirtland's warbler breeds in only a few counties in northern Michigan. The Michigan Department of Natural Resources sponsors tours twice a day during breeding season. This is the final tour of the year. It's me and a group of Seventh Day Adventists. The women are wearing floral print dresses, the men are in black wingtips. The Kirtland's is endangered because of its exact breeding requirements—young jack pine forests growing on a special type of sandy soil. The trees must be of a certain height—between five and sixteen feet tall—and spaced to let sunlight through to the ground. In the past, fire produced these conditions. Now active management of about 140,000 acres of public land has made it possible to stabilize the Kirtland's populations.

We caravan behind our guide to a remote, unnamed location and set out along a hot, dusty trail. We can hear the bird, but for the first hour, he stays hidden. The guide is afraid that it might be too hot and too late in the day, but finally, we spot a female sitting in a tree. A few minutes later a male appears and gives us good views as he sings. On the way back to the hotel, the guide leads me to a second location where he thinks I will be able to add another life bird to my list. And, indeed, a clay-colored sparrow is singing from the exact tree that my guide had predicted.

In 1971, the population of Kirtland's warblers was estimated at 400. Today, it has rebounded to an estimated 1,400. Its existence is precarious, though, dependent on a continuing human commitment to managing forests in its interest. There is a finite number of these precious little birds, and if we aren't careful, we will lose them. Our lives have real limits, too. We don't go around thinking about how many more breaths we will draw, or how many times our hearts will beat, but each is limited. Lovers are only allotted a certain number of kisses. The problem is that we don't know what the limits are. On the morning of November 12, I did not know that Joe's allotment of heartbeats was down to the thousands or that we had just used up our stock of kisses.

Airplanes are literally falling out of the sky as I drive into Traverse City, Michigan. It's Cherry Festival week and the Blue Angels have been hired to entertain the crowds. Sarah's family has had an orchard here for generations and she is spending the summer. When she picks me up at the airport, a Blue Angel thunders overhead. She's horrified that this is how I'm greeted. As we drive farther out the peninsula to the orchard, we leave the noise behind. The countryside is idyllic. Pulling off onto the dirt road that leads to her home, I say to her, "I'm going to try not to say this too much, but it just kills me that Joe is not here to experience this with us."

We spend a lazy day on Friday, part of it on a beach on Lake Michigan that is just a few hundred yards from the house. On Saturday, we venture into town for errands. Unfortunately, the Blue Angels are back. One arcs silently and then accelerates, breaking the sound barrier directly above us. Sarah screams and grabs my arm.

Joe and I came to Michigan twice. The second time, we almost didn't return. We came for a Christmas sing-along at Rosemary and Elliott's. After a potluck supper we sang all of the traditional carols. One of the highlights of the night was when my cousin Andy and his wife Amy, by far the most accomplished singers of the group, were coaxed into singing by themselves. They chose "O Holy Night," Joe's favorite carol.

The following evening, we drove out to Ann Arbor to visit with my cousin Ed and his wife Karen. We had dinner in their home and they surprised Joe with a birthday cake in honor of his thirty-sixth birthday. They also presented him with a hastily-arranged gift—a CD of Luciano Pavarotti's rendition of "O Holy Night" and other carols.

We left Ed and Karen's and began the drive back to Dearborn. Elliot worked for Ford Motor Company and he was driving a new Lincoln Continental. We had been on State Highway 14 for about ten minutes when the car ran onto the soft shoulder of the passing lane. As Elliot tried to get the car back onto the road it began to swerve. Joe and I were in the backseat and could not see what was happening, but suddenly the rear of the car swung forward and we were traveling sideways down the road. In an instant, it flipped over. One whole flip and then another half. The car came to rest upside down on the side of the road, facing oncoming traffic.

We crawled out the back window and gathered by the side of the road. We realized two things: we were okay, and we had been incredibly lucky. The car was totaled. Everything that had not been strapped down was strewn about. My coat was under the car. Rosemary's was wrapped around the front wheel. Three of us had lost our glasses.

Over the next hour we lived out the kind of nightmare you tend to believe only happens to others. First the waiting on a cold, dark road, not knowing when help would arrive. Then the full-blown scene— flashing lights, flares, squawking radios, and passing cars slowing down to stare. We also experienced acts of human kindness. Half a dozen people stopped to help. They brought us flashlights and blankets. They took the coats off their backs and put them around us.

Rosemary would spend two nights in the hospital; the rest of us were sent home. We were all stunned by this near-death experience. I was particularly troubled because I had not worn my seat belt the first time I drove in Elliot's car. From the backseat, the car seemed big and secure, and I knew Elliott was a careful driver. Fortunately, I decided to wear my seat belt on this trip. Had I not, I would have certainly been thrown from the car and killed.

The description of what actually happened comes from Elliott, and by seeing the evidence after the fact. Neither Joe nor I had a full memory of the accident. I blacked out at the point when the car began to pitch forward and came back to consciousness only when I had found a way out through the back window. Joe remained conscious for a little longer; he remembered a sensation of the car rolling over. He also remembered thinking that he was going to die. Then he blacked out.

The accident was a terrifying experience and a frightening lesson in how tenuous our grip on life is. In the immediate aftermath of Joe's death, though, I found myself thinking a lot about that dark Michigan night and taking comfort from two things I learned. The first was that Joe reacted to terror by blacking out. This gave me hope that he reacted in the same way to the terror of Flight 587 spinning out of control. The second lesson was that in moments of terror we think primarily of ourselves. I would like to report that when I came to in the car my first thought was for the safety of Joe and Rosemary and Elliot. I would like to think that as I began to crawl out, I reached over to pull Joe along with me. I did not. I did call out, "this way," but my goal was to get myself out of the car, and only then to think about helping others. I think this is the normal reaction of our brain to danger and, again, this provides some comfort. I hope that in his last moments, Joe was not troubled by thoughts of what would happen to me, or any other issues. I hope that the primordial part of his brain took over and ushered him into unconsciousness.

July 8

Lake Michigan, aboard the SS *Badger* between Ludington, Michigan, and Manitowoc, Wisconsin. I find a lounge chair on the front deck. As we pull out of the harbor I lean up against the side of the boat. The wall comes up to my chest. I rest my arms on top of it and my chin on my arms. It feels very private. Hundreds of people are on the boat, but no one is leaning against the bow like I am, so no one can see me. I say the Serenity Prayer. I'm thinking again about the last minutes of Flight 587. I say to Joe. "It seems like every time I start out on a new journey, I have to relive your last one. I'm so sorry that you had to go through that. I'm so sorry that you had to go through that without me." I don't wish I had died with Joe, but I hate that he had to go through that without me being physically present. How can two people share such a deep connection and yet be so violently and instantly separated? Each partner is required to go through a profound life experience without the other.

July 9

Sturgeon Bay, Wisconsin. Walking through the meadow by the inn where Dwight, Ben, and I are staying, a red-winged blackbird follows me, actively calling and whistling. Each time I advance twenty yards or so, he flies to a tree ahead of me and resumes his calls. They are vociferous defenders of territory. It is not unusual to see them harassing crows to drive them away from their nests. A few times he flies right over my head and clucks. He is most likely trying to keep me away from a nest, but the association of birds with Joe is so strong I let myself wonder if this is Joe with a message for me. What message, though? I had started thinking of this trip as my first vacation without Joe—excluding the ash-scattering trips. Finally, after I have walked several hundred yards, accompanied by the same bird, I turn and face him and ask, "Are you trying to tell me that this is not really the first vacation without you? That I am not really alone?" The blackbird clucks a few times and then settles onto the top of a bush and stops following me.

July 10

Preparing to return to New York today, I take a private minute in the garden. The trip has been very good for me, but this morning has been sad. I say the Serenity Prayer and then speak directly to Joe. "Good morning, my love. I miss you so much. I so wish you were here to enjoy the beauty of this garden with me." I am thinking about a phrase Lorraine used in the letter she wrote supporting my claim for Joe's workers compensation benefits. She referred to me as Joe's "eternal soul mate." I tell this to Joe. "I think she is right. There was something in our meeting beyond chance. We both knew from the beginning that we should be together. There was something that kept us together. I want to believe that we will be connected, no matter what direction my life goes in. Okay?" From behind, a red-winged blackbird, perhaps the same one that escorted me yesterday, answers back with a few clucks.

– XXVI –

From the beginning, death has woven itself into my bird-watching experiences. On a Saturday in late March 1998 I bought a pair of binoculars at Westside Camera on Broadway and set out on my first expedition. I checked the grounds at Morningside Gardens, expecting to find only pigeons (officially called rock doves, according to my new field guide), starlings, and the ubiquitous little brown birds whose name (house sparrow) I did not yet know. With just a few sweeps of my binoculars, though, I was focused in on something red. A candy wrapper—I assumed—until it started to move and revealed itself to be a bird. It was about the size of a pigeon; the red turned out to be a crescent-shaped spot on the bird's nape. When it turned around I saw a triangular patch of black on its breast. Its belly was a light brown and flecked with dark spots. It was beautiful, almost exotic.

The bird lifted itself up in flight, revealing a deep yellow on the undersides of its wings, and flew to a nearby tree. I ran back down the block and found it in my glasses. It rested for a few seconds, giving me a good look, then took off again. The afternoon sun further magnified the brilliance of the yellow under its wings. I had approached this new hobby somewhat tentatively, reluctant to expend the energy it would take to do well, and uncertain about its rewards—just how interesting could looking at birds be? I had my answer quicker than I expected. I had witnessed true beauty, and just yards from my front door in Manhattan. I followed the bird as it propelled itself forward with quick, powerful bursts of its wings. It crossed the street and headed south. Then I saw it desperately flapping its wings and reeling backward. For a moment I thought I was watching a cartoon. Lowering my binoculars, I saw that it had flown directly into a large window at Jewish Theological Seminary. It lay on the sidewalk.

I turned away, feeling that I was intruding on a private moment—the moment of its death. When I returned to my apartment several hours later, the bird was gone. I assumed its body had been cleared away by a building porter, or perhaps a predator. I didn't know then that birds sometimes survived these accidents. It may have only been stunned and flown away when it regained consciousness. Later in the day I spoke with my friend Brad, who had also recently taken up birding. I had by then identified the bird as a northern flicker, a common type of woodpecker, and told him what I had witnessed. At the end of the conversation he asked me where Joe was. I responded that he was due in that evening. It wasn't until I said the words that the significance of Joe being in the air hit me.

I was a bit spooked by the inauspicious start to my new hobby. When I reported to Rosemary and Elliott that I had made the first few entries on a life list, I opted not to mention the ill-fated flight of the flicker. Any birder quickly recognizes the fragile nature of an individual bird's life and how easily it can be extinguished. Had I not turned the event into a story, it certainly would have faded from my memory. Instead, it stayed alive over the next year and a half as I worked on what would eventually become "Widow's Watch." I used my flicker experience and gave the narrator, George, a long-term partner, Ray, who flew for a living. Ray was in the air at the exact moment of the bird's crash and George's fear for his fate becomes the main element of tension in the story:

> Ray flew for a living, and in their twenty-two years together George had had a lot of time to think about flying. Especially at night, when Ray was late getting home, he would ponder the mysteries of flight. How was it possible that an aluminum tube sitting on the ground in some distant location could lift itself up, hurtle through the atmosphere, and come to rest safely in the desired location—a strip of asphalt on the outer edges of Queens? Even if there was a convincing mechanical explanation for how it was done, wasn't it tempting fate to do it repeatedly, to make it routine, to earn a living at it in the same way that George sat at a computer all day and at the end of the month collected a pay-

check, accrued vacation, and provided for retirement and twice-yearly dental visits?

Planes went down; that was certain. The only question was which one? Generally his fears ran along these lines: if Ray's plane did go down it would be out of complacency. It would not be any one individual's fault, but rather the result of a general lackadaisical attitude, the acceptance as commonplace of something that really was extraordinary. Sometimes his thoughts took a darker turn as he tried to fathom the minds of the Saddam Husseins of the world. Weighing the competing threats of international and domestic terrorism, he would suggest route changes to Ray. George knew that such suggestions were futile, but that did not stop him from spinning them out.

Much of this is also autobiographical, born out of late nights waiting for Joe to return and my fears about terrorism. George correctly predicts the nature of Joe's death. He survived September 11 only to succumb to what George regarded as complacency—"the acceptance as commonplace of something that really is extraordinary." This is the bargain we all make every time we step in a plane, a car, or a high-rise building. The vast majority of times, we return without incident. That Joe did not return safely is a profound tragedy, but his death by flying was not foretold on March 28, 1998, when I witnessed a flicker fly into Jewish Theological Seminary. (Why did it have to be a seminary?) The two incidents stand side by side, mysteriously similar, worthy of pondering, but in the end, connected, I believe, only by the mind's need to impose patterns on a random world.

If you were a Colima warbler stopping for a drink from the Rio Grande on your annual journey northward, the Chisos Mountains of Big Bend National Park would seem like the perfect place to raise a family. At least that's how it struck me as Joe and I stood by the river one morning in May 2001 contemplating the precipitous rise of the Chisos from the desert floor. Warblers are the crown jewels of the birding world. At five and three-quarter inches long, the Colima is one of the largest. It weighs in at a third of an ounce. In the United States, it can be found only in the Chisos Mountains. Annual census of breeding populations range from a low of forty-six pairs to a high of eighty-three. They arrive in early April, set up housekeeping in oak and pine canyons above 6,000 feet, and depart later in the summer for their wintering grounds in Colima, Mexico. For serious birders, it's a real prize. That's what brought me to Big Bend. And because I was there, Joe was there, too.

We arrived in Dallas late on a Friday, spent Saturday with Lesley Metz, and early Sunday morning flew in a tiny prop plane to the Midland/Odessa Airport. We rented a car and drove four hours south and west to Big Bend National Park. It was as far as either of us had been from civilization. Our cell phone searched without success for a signal. Putting the car radio on seek, we watched the call numbers loop endlessly, hearing only an occasional scratchy hint of a country western song. When we checked into the Chisos Mountain Lodge the clerk handed me a piece of paper. "Call Elliott Valentine," it read. My heart sank. Rosemary and Elliot were to join us in the search of the Colima, but I knew that the note meant that they would not come. The phone call confirmed my fears: my aunt Judy had died the night before of cancer at her home in South Carolina. Instead of setting out from Tucson on the two-day drive to Big Bend, Rosemary and Elliott would be flying east for the funeral.

Joe offered to accompany me to South Carolina, but I decided to stay and complete our mission. We spent Sunday and Monday acclimating ourselves to Big Bend. The birding was spectacular. I quickly added Scott's oriole, gray hawk, white-throated swift, yellow-breasted chat, and varied bunting to my life list. Joe took a liking to the Mexican jays that hung around our cabin hoping for handouts. He called out to them in broken Spanish. We took short hikes in preparation for the daylong outing that might be necessary to find the Colima. Joe paid particular attention to the trail signs that warned about bears. He practiced the suggested steps: Wave arms, make noise, throw stones.

In the middle of the night before we set out in search of the Colima, I woke up in fear. I had been concerned about Rosemary and Elliott being able to make the hike, but now that it was finally here, I worried about Joe and me. I had never before been in a place where I had such a profound awareness of my status as a visitor. Beyond the cozy confines of the lodge was a potentially hazardous environment. At the farthest point, we would be four miles from the lodge with no means of communication. The trails were steep and rocky. It was conceivable that we would not see another human being along the way. In my mind, I turned over different scenarios. If one of us were injured, what would be worse—to be the one hurt, or the one who had to go get help? I was awake for an hour or so. Joe's sleep did not appear to be troubled by any of this. A patch of moonlight spread across his bed covers. If he dreamed of anything, it was probably of the breakfast buffet that awaited us.

We were up before sunrise and first in line at the door to the restaurant. There were a few big tour buses in the parking lot and it was important that we beat their customers to the buffet line if we were to get an early start on the trail. By seven-thirty we set out, carrying two quarts of water, trail snacks, and lunch. The initial climb was easy, the trails wide and well maintained. By 9 a.m. we began to hear the Colima's song. Shortly after we encountered a man and a woman who were also looking for the elusive bird. The man carried a large camera and tripod in hopes of photographing it. Around 10 a.m. Joe and I were focused in on a pair of gnatcatchers, trying to determine if they were black-tailed, which would be a life bird for me, or blue-gray, which would not. From behind us a voice called out, "Here's your bird." We turned and found the man with the camera setting up his tripod. On a branch of a pine tree, perhaps twenty feet in from the edge of the trail, a bird was singing. We hurried closer for a better view. Once we were away from the chatter of the gnatcatchers, we could hear the distinctive trill of the Colima. The bird was in shadow, though, so other distinguishing features were difficult to see. I was able to make out the eye ring, and the overall drab color. The faint red cap and the orange-toned undertail coverts were impossible to detect from the view we had. The bird granted us a few more seconds viewing time before flying away.

We could have turned around and gotten back to the lodge in time for lunch, but decided to complete the full loop. We continued up Laguna Meadows trail to Colima trail. From there we connected to Boot Canyon trail, where we stopped and had a picnic lunch. We heard several Colimas calling along Boot Canyon, but we were unable to see them. Finally, we headed down the Pinnacles trail, a steep, winding, rock-strewn path that took us back to the trailhead where we had started. We had been gone for over seven hours and had traveled approximately nine miles. I had no more sightings of the Colima, but I decided to put it on my life list.

A week later, Rosemary and Elliott came through. They climbed Laguna Meadow trail and at about noon identified the Colima.

I found the following entry in the notebook I carried with me on our Big Bend trip: "Joe likes birding, but thinks all day about what he is going to have for dinner. Bill likes eating, but spends the meal thinking about what bird he will see next." It's a fairly accurate summary of our differing approaches to bird watching. In 1998 I gave Joe his own pair of binoculars for Christmas. From that point on, we always worked birding trips into our vacations. Twice we hired a guide to show us around Central California birding hot spots. (The first time we hired him Joe asked, "How do we know he's not going to take us out to the woods and kill us?") At home, we took frequent jaunts on weekends to prime birding locations—Jones Beach, Jamaica Bay, Doodletown Road, and Central, Prospect, and Riverside Parks.

Joe always remained an in-the-moment birder. He kept no life list and generally left the identification to me. He did come to love birds. He reacted to them the same way he reacted to cats and children. He delighted in their existence, proclaiming, "sooooo pretty!" or "sooooo cute!" when he had one in his binoculars. Sometimes he addressed them with a personal nickname. cedar waxwings became "see da waxwings." The tufted titmouse became "Tuftie." The cardinal became "José Cardinal" The junco, "Señor el Junco," the J pronounced like a Y, as it would be in Spanish. Mergansers and hermit thrushes became "Mergie" and "Hermie." When we saw a sora, he proclaimed in an outer-borough accent, "I sor a sora!" When I told him I had seen a plain chachalaca in Texas, he replied "A chacha whatcha?" Robins caused him to burst into "A Spoonful of Sugar" or "Rockin' Robin." Not all birds were worthy of praise; the starling was a particularly egregious example of an imported species that has wrecked havoc on certain native species. On encountering a starling, Joe would imitate Jerry Seinfeld's derisive way of greeting Newman, the post office employee. Instead of "Hello, Newman" he would leer "Hello, Starling."

Joe went out birding only twice on his own. Once was on the grounds of Morningside Gardens, where a patrol car pulled up shortly after he had started and the officer asked him what he was doing. Someone had called in a Peeping Tom. (I have birded the grounds at Morningside many times without incident.) The second time was in England, on one of his London layovers. He bought himself a field guide to the birds of England and Europe and began a small life list on a piece of stationary from the Forum Hotel. Among his favorites were the robin, whose face and chest is a striking orange, the mistle thrush, who must have reminded him of his beloved hermit thrush, and the blue tit, whom he probably loved on the basis of the name alone. When he returned from England, he triumphantly sat me down and showed me each of his finds in the field guide.

Joe was a great bird scout. Some of the entries on my life list would not be there if he had not been with me to find them. He picked a great horned owl out of a tree in Morro Bay State Park. He found a much smaller owl, the northern saw-whet, in a pine tree in Central Park. He helped me find the canyon wren along the Window Trail at Big Bend. We had been hearing the haunting call echoing off the steep cliffs, but couldn't match the bird with the song until we were nearly at the end of the trail. While he had a good eye, his preference was for the birds to come to him. Following our Big Bend journey we spent two days in the mountains of southeast Arizona. We went to a bed-and-breakfast in Miller Canyon that catered to birders and sat at a shaded picnic table near a group of hummingbird feeders. We raised our binoculars only when a hummer was spotted at one of the feeders. "This is my kind of birding," Joe remarked.

His last life bird came on September 23, the day after Dianne Snyder's memorial service. Joe, Brad, and I went to the north woods of Central Park. The spell of achingly beautiful fall days continued and the woods were full of birds. Everywhere we turned, something fluttered about. It was reassuring after nearly two weeks of watching and rewatching planes slam into the World Trade Center towers to see flight that was natural, beautiful, and effortless. We walked through a section of the park known as the Loch and at one point I trained my glasses on a branch of a tree by the stream. At first I thought I was looking at a blue jay, but the pattern on the underside of the tail was not right for a jay and the bill was curved. This got my attention. Depending on the color of the lower half of the bill, I may have been looking at a life bird. It was yellow. Yes! "Yellow-billed cuckoo," I called out. Brad and Joe resisted. "No. It's just a blue jay." There was a jay in the same tree and I found myself in a familiar birding dilemma, trying to describe the location of a bird without lowering my own glasses. Fortunately, the cuckoo stirred and both Brad and Joe were able to get a look before it flew away. Given Joe's love of *The Sound of Music*, a cuckoo seems a fitting final life bird for him.

I hope to remain a birder for the rest of my life. I am continually surprised at how much pleasure I get from this hobby. It gets me outdoors and gives me reasons to travel to places I would otherwise ignore. It requires patience and discipline, and in doing so, teaches me the value of both. It provides lessons in the fragility of life, but also in its endurance and resilience. Wherever I bird, I will take Joe with me. I am a better birder because of him. The way we birded reflected the way we worked together in general. Birding started out as mine, but became ours. I brought planning and organization to it. To my form, he added content. Because of Joe, I will always be more appreciative of the birds themselves. I will savor their beauty, call out to them, name them, look upon them with childlike wonder, and thank them for gracing me with their presence.

The American Birding Association's North American Checklist is composed of more than 800 birds. I'm just shy of halfway. It saddens me deeply that Joe will not be present as I make my way through the next 400. He wouldn't have gone with me on every trip, but on those he missed, he would have waited anxiously for my report when I returned home. I don't know how close to 800 I'll get; I've already gotten most of the easy ones. The second 400 is always tougher, and it will be harder still without my trusted scout at my side.

– XXVII –

Lake Winnipesaukee, New Hampshire

The tradition has always been that arriving parties pull into the parking lot at Shep Brown's Boat Basin or the Y landing and call from the pay phone to the cottage on Bear Island. It's just a few minutes by boat from my parents' dock to the mainland. There was a period of time, dating back at least to the 1970s, when pay phones in New Hampshire required that you put the dime in after you had dialed the number, not before, and this often created confusion for guests. The solution was that if the phone rang and no one was on the other end, you hopped in the boat and headed to the mainland.

New Hampshire's pay phones have been updated, and the tradition of using the one at the dock at Shep Brown's survives. In August 2001, when I was giving instructions to Lorraine's husband, Nick, on how to reach us, I told him to pull up to the phone at the public dock and call us. There was a pause at the other end of the line. "Couldn't I just call you from my cell phone as we get close?" he asked. Oh. Well, yes, I guess he could. The thought had never occurred to me. This summer, as I was leaving for the lake, I called the cottage and gave my brother Jim my best estimate of when I would be arriving. Remembering my experience from last year, I told him I would call from my cell phone as I approached. Another pause. "Or just call from the pay phone at the dock," he offered. "Okay," I responded, chuckling. The pull of tradition is very strong at Lake Winnipesaukee.

So strong, perhaps, that it exerted an influence on me as I packed the car. I forgot to remove the cell phone from my bag. It was in the trunk as I approached the lake. This turned out to be a good thing; I needed some time by myself when I arrived. I parked, opened the sunroof, and looked out at the sky. I didn't do anything here that I hadn't done elsewhere. I spoke to Joe; I cried; I sat in silence. My sadness was real and deep, but it existed side by side with a feeling of gratitude. How lucky we were to have had a place like this to share. I felt as I had at Wilbur Hot Springs. The memories were overwhelmingly happy and the sheer physical beauty of the place required that I go forth in good spirits. I went to the trunk, unpacked my cell phone, and called the cottage.

Over the years Joe and I spent a few holiday weekends here with the whole family, but most of our visits were for a week when we had the place to ourselves. Our most spectacular visit was in 1999, when we came late in September and stayed on to celebrate our nineteenth anniversary. The lake was practically deserted. The water was too cold to swim, but the languid fall afternoons were warm enough to permit lolling around on the dock and the evenings were cool enough to draw us to the fireplace.

It took awhile for Joe to feel comfortable coming here. His unease may have been partially caused by his unfamiliarity with boats. Initially, I did all the driving; eventually he became comfortable behind the wheel. It was a standing joke that every time we visited the lake a new part of the boat would be damaged. We did have a string of four years in a row where the propeller, battery, stern light, and side vent had to be replaced. I was responsible for most of it, but Joe feared that we would eventually be banned from the lake. My father was always gracious. "It happens to everyone," he said, trying to reassure him.

Joe liked to call Lake Winnipesaukee "Golden Pond." We rented the movie, which was filmed nearby, several times while we were here. He did a great imitation of Katharine Hepburn. "Norman, the loons," he would warble. Or, "Norman, you old poop!" We established other traditions. A canoe trip down the island was required, as were several visits to a restaurant called Tamarack for lobster rolls or fried clams. We made annual pilgrimages to the Burlwood Antique

Center where we collected paintings and Blue Ridge Pottery, and to a small shop in Center Harbor where we assembled a large collection of green Depression glass. Locally baked blueberry pies were essential to the experience.

This year, I arrive with two cups of ashes. Late on Saturday afternoon we gather on the dock. It's been overcast all day, but the sun finally breaks through just before we begin. There is a "Joe" bench on the dock. Each branch of my family is represented. The kids range from age five to thirteen. They've been given the option to attend or not, and I'm glad that they have chosen to be here. I open up a bottle of wine and pass it around. I pass around the ashes, too. Several of the adults offer stories about Joe. I read Sandburg's "For You" and throw the ashes off the side of the dock. The ashes spread out and form an eerie cloud that slowly sinks to the bottom.

If my earlier visit to California reconfirmed my essential link to Joe's family, this ceremony confirms how tightly woven into the fabric of my family Joe remains. We linger in the late afternoon sun, taking pictures, and trading stories. As if Joe were up there pulling the curtains, the sun retreats behind the clouds as we move slowly toward the cottage for dinner.

On Sunday my siblings and their families begin to leave for home. This is the week Joe and I would have had; I've decided to stay for two nights on my own. Late in the afternoon, I take the last boatload to the mainland. I drive into town to shop, buying a steak and squash to grill for dinner, and a bottle of wine. The lake is calm when I return and I successfully manage to dock the boat by myself. The evening passes peacefully. I decide to sleep in the same bed that Joe and I always slept in. As I turn in, I laugh, thinking of the little ritual we used to go through. The bed has an electric blanket with dual controls. Joe would always set his side to 4 or 5. I would leave mine off.

Monday passes happily, too. The day is largely given over to a jigsaw puzzle. On Tuesday, before I leave, I carry the wooden urn that has held Joe's ashes out to the woodpile and take an ax to it. I lay the pieces in the fireplace and put a match to them. Slowly, as I work at my puzzle, the urn disappears. I still have a sizeable stash of ashes at home. They will be buried with a tree that I will plant at Morningside Gardens. I have set aside three small chunks of bone, but other than that, I will not keep any of Joe's remains. I'm profoundly grateful that I had them. Their existence, and the question of how to dispose of them, helped organize my grief and made the process a more communal one. In the end, though, I need to let go of them. If Joe's death taught me anything, it is how little we control in this world. His spirit lives on, in my heart and many others. It's better that his remains be out there, too.

– XXVIII –

All things end. Joe's life. Our relationship. This writing project. Eventually my life will end, the how and when revealed only as it happens. Without an endpoint our lives make no sense. Whether each individual end is part of a grand design, and whether that end represents a beginning of another sort, is not for us to know.

Our job on earth is to live with uncertainty, ambiguity, and hope. We are given a limited tool set but one, in my opinion, sufficient for the job. Sufficient to allow us to be engaged in life—to love, grieve, work, play, celebrate, and despair. We have a remarkable ability to rebound and grow. We have been granted the capacity for wonder and laughter, most important at ourselves. These last two gifts were bestowed generously on Joe and he, in turn, taught me how vital they are.

Much of my work over the past ten months has centered on reorganizing my physical surroundings. Joe would not be surprised by this. He used to call me "Mr. Infrastructure" because of all the time I spent in our closets, arranging and rearranging things so that everything fit. Joe had pack-rat tendencies and a high tolerance for clutter. I had to shame him into cleaning up the piles he left behind on the dresser, the desk, chairs, in the sink, and on the floor. It fell to me to enforce—ruthlessly at times—the principle that if something new was brought into the apartment, something old had to go. I took great pleasure in maintaining our infrastructure. I looked at it in the same way that Tony Lopes looked at thinking. An ongoing, unceasing ebb and flow of objects was around us and in their management I found a deep consolation. Was this one worth keeping? Where did it fit? What did it say about us? The questions applied to everything that came into the apartment, whether an oil painting or a can of soup.

With Joe's death, everything was in question again. What stays? What goes? Who gets what? In one sense, it's easier because I can make all of the decisions. I still have the old arguments in my head, but in the end I win. Dividing his things into collections and appointing curators has helped turn a dreary task into an enjoyable one. It made me very happy to spread his things among friends and family.

There are some surprises. Joe's underwear is gone, while his albums, whose removal I championed for years, are still here. From the beginning I feared dealing with his stack of briefs—so sensual, boyish, and erotic. So personal. At the same time, I was having my own underwear issues, with two loads coming out yellow from the washing machine. Initially I felt as if I was operating under a laundry room curse, punishment, perhaps, for having lived so long off of Joe's talents. Then I saw that the staining of my briefs could make it easier to dispose of Joe's. I mixed my yellow ones in with his and threw the whole bunch down the chute. Our briefs did what we couldn't do— go out together.

Meanwhile, the albums sit on the bottom shelf of a bookcase. They will go some day, but I am in no hurry. I like looking at them and thinking about all of the various sides of Joe they reveal (John Philip Sousa or Melba Moore?). I have simplified the organization of music in the apartment. The turntable and tape deck have been removed; there is less clutter. Joe didn't care that his music was spread out over 45s, LPs, tapes, and CDs and that this required a big tangle of wires. All that mattered was that he had access to his music when he needed it. It's not that I'm oblivious to the content of the collection, but I can't think about something without thinking about its organization as well. It comforts me to have pared down to just CDs and to have brought order to the armoire.

All of this has helped me through this time of loss. The writing, traveling, ash scattering, organizing photographs, emptying closets, and legal challenges have given structure and meaning to the process of grieving Joe's death. It wasn't just busy work in order to avoid the pain; many times it took me straight into the pain. But I have rarely felt stuck there. A great void remains at the center of my life, but my life does not feel empty.

Is there a point, then, when my grieving is done? Another way the question posed itself to me this summer was, Is my work on earth with Joe done? The first time the question occurred to me, I couldn't bear the thought of it and put my hands over my eyes to shut it out. But I think the answer is yes. Grief never ends, but this period of devoting my life to grieving should end. It is only a question of degree; I can no more turn off my feelings of loss or stop thinking of Joe than I could bring him back to life. Nor can I stop living now because of the desire for a reunion with Joe later. Our connection was deep and profound, and if such connections survive death, then it awaits me.

This morning I am blessed with a vivid dream. I am reunited with Joe following the crash. After thinking for several days that he was dead, he turns up in Yonkers, New York. I join him there. The room we are in is white. Sunlight pours through the windows. Some time has passed since our reunion, but we haven't yet talked about all that went on during those few days when I thought I had lost him. I tell him that I want to talk about this so that he knows how I felt about him and what he meant to me. We hold each other and kiss, although we don't actually talk before I wake up. As in previous dreams, he is smiling radiantly at me.

There is much to take solace in here. The dream takes place on the morning of what I had decided would be my final entry in this journal. August 31 is a year to the day from when Joe and I saw Etta James at B. B. King's. It was the last day before September 2001 and all of the world-changing events that ensued. The dream speaks to my fears that Joe did not know the depth of my love for him when he left this world. His response to my saying that we need to talk is simply to smile and embrace me. No words are necessary. Perhaps he is also saying that no more writing is necessary, in effect confirming my decision to end this memoir.

Even Yonkers makes sense to me. We passed a small bungalow along the Saw Mill River Parkway in Yonkers when we traveled north. Joe would often comment on it, saying that it was the kind of house he would like to own and fix up. I think in his mind the perfect little bungalow represented home, that mythical place where we at last feel settled. Perhaps he has found his little bungalow. Perhaps on November 12 he was called home.

Like the dream at the six-month anniversary and the dreams I had in December, the timing of this one is notable, as is the way in which it speaks directly to my concerns. The dreams are like the birds—the red-tailed hawks outside our building, the calliope hummingbirds' unprecedented arrival in Manhattan last November, Rosemary's seven-hundredth life bird as she prayed for us, the hermit thrush on the grounds as I went to sign papers for the apartment, and, most recently, the red-winged blackbird in Wisconsin clucking in response to my questions. Dreams and birds alike arrive, convey their message, and depart. They are just wisps, shrouded in mystery, but they bear hope for a lasting connection with Joe.

In my letter at the beginning of this writing project, I asked a series of questions. Why you? Why now? How could you survive September 11 and then have this happen? How could American Airlines lose three planes within a two-month period? Why has your family had to endure the loss of its mother and two gay sons? Why you instead of me? I knew that I would never answer these questions, but hoped that in my writing a new perspective might emerge.

In a sense it has. Writing has given me a longer view and helped me see that Joe's death is only part of a larger mystery. What brought the window crashing down on my teammate's head to give me an opening line at the baths on the night we met? What sent a wave circling around us at the beach on our second night as if to baptize our relationship? What caused me to pick up the phone and call Joe in Chicago to tell him I loved him the morning after he had spent the night with another man? What led me to finally rebel against the DWP so that I would be expelled just as Joe had reached his limit?

These, too, are unanswerable questions, but they point to a larger truth. The mystery of Joe's death must be considered in light of our whole relationship. If it began in mystery and was sustained by mysterious interventions, is it so surprising that it ended as it did? Mystery deepens our understanding and appreciation of life. Should I not, then, look hopefully toward my future, wondering what awaits me in the years I have been granted beyond Joe's life?

Another ending, dear boy, which is to say another beginning. The word "good-bye" catches in my throat and every time I think this is what I am saying by ending this writing, I rebel. The truth is I have already crossed that bridge. We said good-bye on the morning of November 12. How fortunate I am that we parted happily, and that "I love you" were the last words I heard from you.

An e-mail today from Janet is full of news of her first semester at San Francisco State—your alma mater—and of how she and Kevin are settling into the house you lived in when we met. She is busy with wedding plans. Isn't it wonderful how life goes on, how a new generation comes along and plunges into life without fear? Again, how fortunate I am to be a part of this.

I love you, Joe Lopes. I have written that you were the best thing that ever happened to me, but I also know now that the reverse is true. We each were exactly what the other needed. We did as well as two people could do together. I know that I have your blessing to love again, should I be lucky enough to find someone to love. It is the best way I can honor our relationship and the love you bestowed so abundantly upon me.

I know, too, that I am free to live fully and joyfully. I have adopted the title song from one of our favorite CDs by Djivan Gasparyan as my motto: "I Will Not Be Sad in This World." This is the best way I can honor and preserve the legacy of joy you bequeathed to us all.

I have been thinking about "Under the Harvest Moon" this morning. It's one of the Carl Sandburg poems that Curtis read at your service. "Death, the gray mocker, / Comes and whispers to you / As a beautiful friend who remembers." And then: "Love, with little hands, / Comes and touches you / With a thousand memories, / And asks you / Beautiful, unanswerable questions." I'm also thinking of a line from

Tony's journal: "Joy can sear like grief." And of the poem that Lorraine entered into his journal after he died: "Suddenly I realized / That if I stepped out of my body I would break / Into blossom."

Have you broken into blossom, Joe? I broke down several times this morning as I labored to finish this. It's hard to tell if it's the old pain or something different, like a shedding of skin to give way to the new. Is it death and its thousand memories whose presence I feel, or love with its unanswerable questions? Why is it so hard to tell the difference? Is it because beauty accompanies them both? (There was great beauty in your death, Joe—in the memorial service, in the outpouring of love and support, even in grief itself, so intensely felt.) When I cried this morning it felt as it had in the past—the tears, the ache in the gut, the clutch in the throat—but also different. There was an unfamiliar sensation in my upper body, a lightness in my shoulders and arms. Even as I sobbed, I felt a desire for release. I couldn't tell where grief ended and joy began.

ABOUT THE AUTHOR

Bill Valentine lives in Manhattan. As of this writing, Ollie and Loretta are still with him. This is his first published full-length work. More to come.

Order a copy of this book with this form or online at:
http://www.haworthpress.com/store/product.asp?sku=5542

A SEASON OF GRIEF

_____in softbound at $14.95 (ISBN-13: 978-1-56023-573-6; ISBN-10: 1-56023-573-X)

Or order online and use special offer code HEC25 in the shopping cart.

COST OF BOOKS_____

☐ **BILL ME LATER:** (Bill-me option is good on US/Canada/Mexico orders only; not good to jobbers, wholesalers, or subscription agencies.)

☐ Check here if billing address is different from shipping address and attach purchase order and billing address information.

POSTAGE & HANDLING_____
(US: $4.00 for first book & $1.50 for each additional book)
(Outside US: $5.00 for first book & $2.00 for each additional book)

Signature_____

SUBTOTAL_____

☐ **PAYMENT ENCLOSED: $_____**

IN CANADA: ADD 7% GST_____

☐ **PLEASE CHARGE TO MY CREDIT CARD.**

STATE TAX_____
(NJ, NY, OH, MN, CA, IL, IN, PA, & SD residents, add appropriate local sales tax)

☐ Visa ☐ MasterCard ☐ AmEx ☐ Discover
☐ Diner's Club ☐ Eurocard ☐ JCB

Account # _____

FINAL TOTAL_____
(If paying in Canadian funds, convert using the current exchange rate, UNESCO coupons welcome)

Exp. Date_____

Signature_____

Prices in US dollars and subject to change without notice.

NAME_____

INSTITUTION_____

ADDRESS_____

CITY_____

STATE/ZIP_____

COUNTRY_____ COUNTY (NY residents only)_____

TEL_____ FAX_____

E-MAIL_____

May we use your e-mail address for confirmations and other types of information? ☐ Yes ☐ No
We appreciate receiving your e-mail address and fax number. Haworth would like to e-mail or fax special discount offers to you, as a preferred customer. **We will never share, rent, or exchange your e-mail address or fax number.** We regard such actions as an invasion of your privacy.

Order From Your Local Bookstore or Directly From
The Haworth Press, Inc.
10 Alice Street, Binghamton, New York 13904-1580 • USA
TELEPHONE: 1-800-HAWORTH (1-800-429-6784) / Outside US/Canada: (607) 722-5857
FAX: 1-800-895-0582 / Outside US/Canada: (607) 771-0012
E-mail to: orders@haworthpress.com

For orders outside US and Canada, you may wish to order through your local
sales representative, distributor, or bookseller.
For information, see http://haworthpress.com/distributors

(Discounts are available for individual orders in US and Canada only, not booksellers/distributors.)

PLEASE PHOTOCOPY THIS FORM FOR YOUR PERSONAL USE.
http://www.HaworthPress.com   BOF04